CREATE A
WILDLIFE
FRIENDLY
GARDEN

Sharon Amos

COLLINS & BROWN

Introduction

With enormous pressure on land for housing and sweeping changes in farming practices, it's little wonder that wildlife is being pushed out of the countryside. But there is still an untapped reserve of land and resources right under our feet.

Domestic gardens make up millions of acres and offer a rich diversity of habitats and varied plantings, and trends in gardening are making our plots much more attractive to wildlife than the artificially boosted green lawns and rows of bedding plants of the past.

The swing towards gardening organically has improved things enormously. Where once the only response to an attack of greenfly was to reach for a chemical solution, and spraying the roses was a regular event in the gardener's calendar, killing off all kinds of insects at once, we're now beginning to see there is another way.

A BALANCING ACT

Gardening is a balancing act: for every insect pest there is a predator and, if we can make small adjustments to garden management to encourage the right predators, then we are well on the way to setting up a garden ecosystem that will take care of itself with minimum intervention.

Cottage-style gardens, with their jumble of flowers and vegetables, fruit trees and rose bushes, and their emphasis on the old, unimproved species of flowers that are full of scent and nectar, are a step in the right direction, as is an interest in companion planting.

A relaxed attitude is important when making a wildlife-friendly garden: learning to accept a clump of nettles here, the odd dandelion there, not rushing to sweep up leaves, mow the lawn every Sunday or hoe off every last weed makes gardening a more easy-going experience and leaves vital resources available to wildlife, as well as giving you more time to sit and watch.

The loss of meadows and hedgerow wildflowers in the wider landscape has had a dire effect on the butterfly population but, by planting flowers for nectar and leaving the odd patch of caterpillar food plants, we can start to reverse the trend. Once your garden really gets going you may be able to spot as many as fifteen to twenty different butterfly species.

The grubbing-out of hedgerows to make bigger fields has reduced nesting and roosting sites for birds, as has the loss of mature trees and old buildings. By introducing a nest box or two into your garden you can start to redress the balance. And it's not just birds that need houses – bats, ladybirds, lacewings and butterflies all need winter shelter too. Also, by feeding birds when food supplies are scarce you'll ensure that they are in the right place – your garden – when insect pests start to build up.

This book doesn't aim to tell you what you will or won't see in your garden – it's not a wildlife guide. It's just full of suggestions of what to grow to attract wildlife and small changes that you can make to your style of gardening that will make big differences to the wildlife visiting your garden. A garden isn't a nature reserve and you can't trust entirely to nature to deal with everything. You're still going to have to interfere, but in a very positive way that has real benefits for wildlife and for gardeners too.

Designing a wildlife friendly garden

Designing and planting a wildlife garden needs a little extra thought and research. Trees, shrubs and flowers need to contribute more to the garden than simply being beautiful to look at. And there are all sorts of neat tricks for creating mini wildlife habitats, from logpiles to ponds.

Plants and management for a wildlife garden

Take a look at your garden from a whole different perspective – that of a wild creature. You need to provide shelter, sources of food and water, and places for breeding.

Trees and shrubs are potential nesting sites and food sources – through fruit and berry production or because of the wide range of insects they support, which in turn are food for birds and small mammals. Assess flowers for their nectar-producing capability, which will attract bees, butterflies and other beneficial insects, or because of the seeds they produce to feed seed-eating birds. You need to consider when plants flower, to keep a near-constant nectar supply from early spring to early winter.

But this doesn't mean that beauty and aesthetics take second place. Flowers that attract beneficial insects are some of our garden favourites; our native shrubs and trees that make the best habitat for birds and small creatures are some of the most attractive that there are. Fortunately their year-round appeal to wildlife coincides with the sort of things we look for in an ornamental garden plant too – beautiful blossom, colourful berries and dense foliage.

There are plenty of simple garden features that we can introduce as positive wildlife benefits without sacrificing style and elegance. Creeper- and climber-clad walls are much more attractive than bare brick or fence panels and, at the same time, create shelter for roosting and nesting birds, and for overwintering insects. A simple rockery or rustic logpile creates habitats for seldom-seen toads, newts and frogs.

Small changes in garden management can make big differences to local wildlife. Leaving seedheads in place for birds, letting patches of nettles grow in odd corners and letting brambles scramble through hedges can all improve the environment for wildlife.

YOUR OWN GARDEN TEMPLATE

The first thing to remember about creating a wildlife-friendly garden is that it is for your enjoyment too.

above The edge of a wood is a wildlife-rich habitat, and one that is easily recreated in a garden.

far right Coneflowers are composed of masses of tiny individual florets, each with its own nectar supply. Tall Brazilian verbena (in the background) also attracts butterflies and insects.

There's no fun in handing the garden over to nature entirely so that you look out of the kitchen window onto a sea of brambles or have to fight your way out of the back door to get to the dustbin.

First decide what you need from the garden and make a list: sunny patio, shady bench, vegetable patch, shed, washing line, a lawn for the children to play on. Then you can work out the wildlife elements that you'd like to add – such as a bird table, nest boxes or a pond – and how the two (your needs and the wildlife elements) are going to interact together.

One of the most successful ways to entice wildlife of all descriptions into your garden is to take note of the surrounding land and then use your garden to complement the encircling habitat. If there are ponds, streams or wetlands nearby, you can be sure that, by building a pond in your garden, wildlife will swiftly colonize it. Woods or mature trees in nearby gardens and parks mean that you can build on what's already close by, planting a tree or two and making a shrubbery that mimics the edge of woodland habitat, so attracting woodland birds into your garden, not to mention small mammals such as bats and squirrels.

Then you can really start to improve on nature by adding nest boxes and a feeding table, making roosting sites and adding a bird bath, and planting a rich variety of nectar and seed-producing plants.

A key element to enjoying a wildlife-friendly garden is to be able to sit and watch what's going on. In good weather this might mean being able to see the pond from the patio while you're sitting having lunch – so that you can watch dragonflies darting and hovering, swallows swooping low to catch insects, the odd frog diving into the pool. In winter you want to be able to see the bird table from a window in the kitchen or sitting room.

Template for a small garden

A small garden can still be a valuable wildlife habitat. Once you've established where you want to sit in the garden, you can start to plan the wildlife elements.

In a city garden where the boundaries are often walls, start by adding a couple of brackets to hold bird feeders as a sure-fire way of getting birds to visit. On another wall, one of the most important things you can do is to add some trellis or wires and plant a climber to cover the wall. This will become a potential nesting site for birds and a place for insects to shelter. If you choose a flowering climber such as honeysuckle, which also produces berries, then you're more than doubling the benefits to wildlife. Adding a nest box (see pages 64–73) in amongst the climber will give birds an additional hint.

OTHER THINGS YOU CAN DO
- Look at the planting in the garden to see if there is space for a small tree.

- If you're building a raised bed, leave a gap or two in the bricks or retaining stones as a hiding place for a toad.

- Work out where the sunniest, most sheltered spot in the garden is and give this area over to making a flowerbed for bees and butterflies.

above right   Make use of every available space. Here even the gaps in the mortar of the steps contain a mixture of container-grown plants and self-seeded plants.

below right   In a small garden you can still gain height by growing tall plants like the Scotch thistle (on the right) and hemp agrimony (on the left), both of which attract insects and birds

- Lawn – if space

- Paved seating area

- Small pond – if space or practical

- Bird bath

- Feeding table

- Nest box

- Climber

- Shrubs

- Tree – if space

- Flowers

Even in a small garden, you can provide valuable nectar plants such as old-fashioned china asters.

Template for an overgrown garden

With an overgrown garden you're almost starting from the opposite perspective, especially when the garden has been neglected for a long time and nature has taken over. What your aim should be is to reclaim some areas for yourself and gradually begin a management plan for the rest of the garden, depending on how big it is.

Where a hedge has grown unchecked it can conceal an awful lot of garden space but at the same time provide good nesting sites. Cutting it back hard in spring before birds start nesting will help rejuvenate it. Use your judgement on how hard to cut it back – if the garden includes other nesting sites, such as ivy and evergreen trees, you can afford to be severe.

Flowering and berried shrubs can often be brought back into full production by hard pruning over several years – take out a third of the old stems at a time, right back to ground level.

Big trees may need remedial work to lift the crown and let light into the garden so that the rest of the planting can thrive. If you are getting in a tree surgeon, choose a sympathetic one who will work with you to leave areas of dead wood for woodpeckers and tree-nesters – provided this doesn't compromise safety, of course.

Clearing border edgings and uncovering paths will quickly bring a sense of order to an overgrown garden, and mowing a patch of grass will give you a good observation point to install a bird table and watch the birds coming and going.

right A tangle of flowers including cosmos and mallow have engulfed this cottage garden, but are perfect for visiting insects.

far right Brazilian verbena, angelica, cardoon thistles and the giant spanish oat grass (Stipa gigantea) have taken over a border with big benefits for birds, butterflies and bees. Old-fashioned roses, honeysuckle and elder will all respond well to hard pruning.

OVERGROWN GARDEN CHECKLIST

- Prune shrubs and trees
- Cut back hedges
- Clear paths
- Thin out pond plants such as water lilies and water iris

Template for a large garden

In a large garden the only constraints are your budget and your imagination.

With extra space to play with you can create a whole spectrum of habitats: hot sunny borders packed with plants to attract bees and butterflies; a pond big enough to entice waterfowl to stay and nest; a woodland glade; or even a reasonable-sized meadow to attract even more wildlife.

Hedges are one of the most important garden elements, providing shelter and food for many different creatures. By planting extra hedges to divide your garden into different areas, you can vastly increase the available shelter and nesting sites for birds and small mammals.

You'll have space to make a big untidy compost heap, to let nettles flourish in a spot not visible from the house, to allow the odd bramble to snake across the hedge. You can let dead branches fall and add to them to make a habitat for toads, frogs and the insects that they eat. You can make a rustic rockery for lizards, slow worms and beetles; let a collapsing shed stay for extra shelter and nest sites.

For days when you don't want to stray far outdoors, have a lawn near the house where you can site a bird table and a bird bath in order to appreciate garden wildlife from the comfort of indoors.

above   A large garden means room for planting on a grand scale, with generous borders of perennial summer flowers, deep, thick hedges and open grassland.

above Use a woodland-edge planting scheme to extend an area of trees in a large garden – foxgloves, ferns and primulas will all thrive.

Wildflowers run riot in an area of garden managed as a summer meadow, with poppies, daisies, cornflowers, sorrel, and wild mustard.

Template for a terrace garden

A city courtyard or paved townhouse garden has plenty of potential to attract wildlife on a small scale. By growing a climber up a wall you can add shelter for birds and insects; and some species of trees and shrubs can even be grown in containers.

A terrace garden will tend to rely on containers and raised beds for planting areas, which are ideal for creating mini habitats. Many butterfly and bee plants grow particularly well in pots, especially sun-loving Mediterranean species like lavender and rosemary that hate to become waterlogged.

By growing bog plants in a sealed, glazed container, you can make a mini wetland that may attract dragonflies. A small pebble water feature that endlessly recirculates water will attract birds and is more decorative than a plain bird bath. Even the simple act of raising a few pots up on bricks can create exactly the right conditions for a toad to live in the damp shade below.

Some small trees can be grown successfully in tubs, as can shrubs. Choose species that offer positive wildlife benefits, such as early spring blossom or autumn berries. Climbers such as clematis and honeysuckle can be grown in tubs too, as can ivy – all of which will add valuable shelter to a small space, as well as nectar and in some cases berries.

It's not impossible to picture a terrace with, say, an ornamental sculpted piece of dead wood that will look interesting as well as providing a habitat for insects that feed on decaying wood.

above   Leopard's bane (*Doronicum* spp.), variegated iris and hellebores can all be container grown, but like all pots will need regular watering.

**PATIO GARDEN
CHECKLIST**

- Birdbath or water feature
- Wall-mounted bird feeder
- Climber
- Raised beds, or pots of bee-and butterfly-friendly flowers raised on bricks
- Tree in a tub
- Berrying shrub in a tub

above   Pots of pansies on a patio table with climbing honeysuckle reaching over from a neighbouring wall. Honeysuckle is an all-purpose wildlife plant, providing nectar followed by berries, plus shelter within its tangle of stems and leaves.

right   A trough of nectar plants for bees and butterflies, including ice plants (*Sedum spectabile*), pinks (*Dianthus* spp.), cranesbill geranium (*Geranium sanguineum*) and creeping thyme (*Thymus praecox*).

below   A terraced-sized trough of nectar plants for bees and butterflies, including ice plants (*Sedum spectabile*), pinks (*Dianthus* spp.), cranesbill geranium (*Geranium sanguineum*) and creeping thyme (*Thymus praecox*).

Template for a balcony garden

While it would be unrealistic to suggest that a balcony can become a wildlife habitat, what it can become is a valuable stopping-off point in various wild creatures' daily routine.

By using clever container planting you can create a succession of just the sort of flowers that bees and butterflies need, just as efficiently as in a full-size border. A trough or tub planted with grape hyacinths and primroses will be a nectar source for the earliest insects on the wing. When these plants die back you can add summer annuals such as marigolds, sweet peas and tobacco plants. Plant containers downwards as well as up and add ivy and other trailing plants to create mini sheltered habitats. Lavender and rosemary do well in pots and if kept neatly clipped can be a decorative feature all year round and not just when they're in flower. If your balcony is very sheltered, you may find that you can actually extend the flowering season beyond that of a conventional flowerbed, with good results for visiting local wildlife.

In some cases you don't even need a balcony. Even a windowbox will attract butterflies if planted with a succession of the right flowers. And birdfood suppliers offer ingenious bird feeders and water containers that attach directly to the window if there's nowhere else to hang a feeder.

right Tiered wooden boxes, used as planters, hold spring plantings of miniature narcissi, crocus, snakeshead fritillaries, spurge, miniature tulips and anemones. When these die back after flowering, annual summer-flowering plants can be carefully tucked in between the bulbs.

far right When space is at a premium, you can use the tops of walls for planting displays.

- Bee and butterfly plants in pots
- Wall-mounted bird feeder or window-mounted feeder/water supply

Above Here a hanging pots of plants have been used effectively to decorate a balcony.

Identifying wildlife friendly plants

Plants can fulfil a whole range of needs for wildlife, from food sources of nectar and berries – or the insects that feed on them – to roosting and nesting sites.

Flowering plants will attract butterflies, bees and other insects in search of nectar and, after they have finished flowering, the seed they set attracts various bird species. Shrubs that produce berries in autumn and winter can provide a valuable food supply for birds; dense, twiggy bushes make good nesting sites. Trees can support many different types of insect, which in turn are food for birds and bats.

NATIVE SPECIES

Wherever possible the golden rule has to be to plant native species. It's common sense really. Wildlife has evolved to make use of the habitat around it, usually with benefits on both sides. Birds get to eat rosehips, and the indigestible seeds within get distributed via their droppings. Bees gather nectar and pollen, inadvertently pollinating the flower in the process so that it can produce fruit or set seeds.

The other rule is to grow plants that are unimproved by breeders and nurseries. Cultivated varieties or cultivars may have frilly petals or double flowers, but their original characteristics – scent, nectar, pollen – have all but disappeared and these were what made them attractive to wildlife such as bees and butterflies in the first place. Very often too, cultivars are sterile and don't produce seed, a blow to seed-eating birds.

WEEDS

Don't worry that your garden will become a less beautiful place. While it helps to start looking at weeds from a fresh viewpoint rather than that of a traditional gardener, there's little point in turning over your garden to the wild. You've got to enjoy it too. Brambles and nettles and elder all have their place in the wildlife garden, but they can be mixed in with all manner of more traditionally acceptable garden plants that have their roots in wild species.

So what constitutes a wildlife-friendly plant? It may be an all-round star, with nectar-filled flowers, berries or seeds for birds, and dense foliage to shelter small creatures; or it may fulfil one vital function in the wildlife garden, such as being a specific caterpillar food plant. The following pages will help you to see plants for what they are.

above Tall pink hemp agrimony (*Eupatorium cannabinum*) is an ideal bee and butterfly plant, as are spiny *Eryngium bourgatti* with its heads of tightly packed blue flowers, and cherry-red *Knautia macedonica*.

right Foxgloves are mainly bee plants as only they can crawl inside the flowers – butterflies just can't reach the nectar source. Simple single roses have open flowers that all insects can access.

Trees and shrubs

Start by looking at the basic framework of your garden – trees and shrubs. If you have space, one of the easiest ways to grow a variety of shrubs is as a boundary hedge. Look for bushes that have winter berries, such as holly and pyracantha. Both species are spiny so will also create a secure garden enclosure.

DUAL-PURPOSE PLANTS

In a small garden where every plant has to earn its keep and there's room for only one or two decorative shrubs, choose species that are at least dual purpose, that is to say have nectar-rich flowers to attract useful insects followed by berries for birds. Shrubs from the genus *Cotoneaster* are ideal: their tiny flowers are popular with bees and later on their berries contribute to birds' winter diet.

HEDGES

Most of us won't have space to grow forest giants such as oak and beech as specimen trees but it is still possible to include them in a garden by making them part of a mixed hedge. Native oaks support an incredible diversity of insect species – close to 300 species – which in turn are food for birds and small mammals. By including them in a run of hedging you really are making a difference to your garden habitat. Beech has long been a favourite for hedges because of its habit of hanging on to its brown autumn leaves, making it a good windbreak and wildlife shelter.

Other trees that lend themselves readily to hedging include hawthorn, field maple and yew. Hawthorn blossom will support a wide range of insects and the berries that follow can form a substantial part of a wild bird's diet. Birds appreciate fleshy red yew berries but these are poisonous to domestic pets, farm animals and humans, so plant yew with discretion – a berry-producing juniper bush can be a better alternative if your garden borders on pastureland.

FRUIT TREES

Fruit trees make good specimen trees in a garden. Bees and gardeners appreciate the blossom and, with a bit of give and take, it should be possible for both gardener and wildlife to benefit from the fruit later in the season. Scientific developments in growing apple trees have produced trees in a range of sizes to suit smaller gardens; and crab apples make compact, wildlife-friendly trees too. Plum trees and their wild cousins, damsons, are manageable garden trees and in a good summer produce more than enough fruit for jam-making and feeding the birds.

BIRCHES

Birch trees are fast growing and, although they grow tall, their slender trunks and open canopy don't generally cause a problem in a small garden. In return you get flocks of seed-eating birds in autumn when the birch catkins release clouds of winged seed and all sorts of birds regularly patrolling in search of insects. Woodpeckers are often attracted to silver birch, especially older trees where there is a decaying branch or two. By buying a multi-stemmed birch you can create a mini woodland glade.

top A rose hedge helps wildlife in a range of different ways: its simple open flowers are insect-friendly and its dense, thorny depths shelter birds, small mammals and insects.

above An apple tree is another multi-purpose wildlife species, producing blossom to attract insects, followed by fruit appreciated by a whole range of wildlife from butterflies and wasps to birds and hedgehogs.

left After a rose bush has finished flowering, the hips provide a ready-made autumn larder for birds.

Butterfly plants

Choose flowering plants carefully and you will attract a wide range of butterflies into your garden in search of high-energy nectar.

Butterflies are highly active insects and need a source of energy to keep them on the wing. They get this from nectar produced by flowers and this is their main reason for visiting gardens.

Plants that attract butterflies tend to be strongly scented, and flower colour seems to play a part too. Butterflies tend to prefer mauves and purples, followed by reds and yellows. They can see a wider spectrum of colours than the human eye, and many blooms have invisible honey guides that point insect visitors in the right direction.

Their long proboscoes or tongues mean butterflies can extract nectar from most flower shapes, especially long, tubular ones. Densely clustered flower heads are best as the butterfly barely has to move as it probes flower after flower – buddleja, valerian, ice plants (*Sedum spectabile*), lavender and marjoram are ideal.

Where plants are growing in the garden has an effect on their butterfly-attracting powers. Butterflies are cold-blooded creatures and their body temperature is governed by the ambient conditions. That's why you see relatively few butterflies on the wing on cool, overcast days, compared to spells of brilliant sunshine. Siting nectar plants in a warm, sheltered, sunny corner practically guarantees they'll be visited constantly.

above right A small tortoiseshell butterfly on a lavender flower spike. On warm days, you can see nectar drops on the flowers.

below right Brazilian verbena (*Verbena bonariensis*) is a relatively new garden plant but its densely packed tubular flowers have been an instant hit with butterflies.

Bee plants

Bees can exploit a bigger range of flowers than butterflies as they are able to crawl inside some blooms to reach the nectar.

As well as visiting flowers to collect nectar, bees are also after pollen, which is rich in protein and fats and is a vital food source for bee larvae being raised in the nest in spring and early summer. The sugar in the nectar is the main energy source for adult bees. Many flowers attract both bees and butterflies but, in addition to those flower types described opposite, bees can crawl into flowers where butterflies would have difficulty reaching the nectar source, such as antirrhinums (snapdragons), salvias and foxgloves.

Always go for the simple, unimproved species when choosing plants for nectar – overbred double flowers very often have all the nectar and pollen, not to mention all the scent, bred out of them. Simple old-fashioned dog roses with flat, open flowers are far more nectar- and pollen-friendly than hybrids packed with petals; plain apple and cherry blossom are more bee-friendly than ornamental pompom-style blooms.

Thistles make great bee or butterfly plants. If you have space, go for the Scotch thistle (*Onopordum acanthium*) or the milk thistle (*Silybum marianum*); in a smaller garden try the closely related knapweed (*Centaurea nigra*) or cornflowers (*Centaurea cyanus*).

To make it productive for bees and butterflies to visit your garden, grow nectar plants in stands or swathes, not dotted about the border so that the insects have to track down each plant.

above right Two-lipped flowers such as salvias are popular with bees, which can crawl in between the two halves to reach the nectar.

below right Stems packed with individual flowers make life easier for bees.

Insect-attracting plants

Boost your garden's population of beneficial insects by planting their favourite flowers.

Look around you as you go for a walk on a summer's day and you'll soon spot which sort of flowers insects prefer. In the hedgerows, cow parsley (*Anthriscus sylvestris*) and hog weed (*Heracleum* spp.) are always alive with hoverflies, beetles, bees and wasps. Both these wildflowers belong to the Umbelliferae family and are characterized by gently rounded flower heads composed of many small individual flowers, their stalks radiating from a single point on the stem like the spokes of an umbrella.

Some gardeners are happy to allow cow parsley into their own garden but in a small plot it can become invasive due to its prolific success at self-seeding. Instead look for more ornamental species from the same family. Fennel is a good example: it has greeny-yellow flower heads popular with all sorts of insects and later on produces a plentiful crop of seeds for the birds. Other ornamental umbellifers include angelica and lovage, two more herb garden plants. In the vegetable plot, try leaving a few carrots to go to seed. You'll spot the resemblance to the Umbelliferae-family immediately, and see how their flowers are like a magnet to insects.

Yarrow (*Achillea* spp.) is another insect-friendly wildflower that has more decorative garden cousins. 'Cloth of Gold' and 'Gold Plate', both cultivars of *Achillea filipendulina*, have great, flat, plate-like flower heads crammed with tiny starry flowers, and look great in the border as well as attracting useful insects.

right The round globes of allium flowers attract useful insects, even though they smell rather oniony.

Caterpillar food plants

A few holes in a few leaves is a small price to pay for the beauty of having butterflies and moths in the garden.

While we all love butterflies, not everyone appreciates caterpillars. Unfortunately you can't have one without the other – and while butterfly food plants are attractive garden plants in their own right, the same isn't always true of caterpillar food plants.

One of the most popular food plants is the stinging nettle (*Urtica dioica*), which is the host plant for four or five species of caterpillar. It should be relatively easy to leave a patch of nettles in the garden: they don't need to be in a prominent position in the border. You've probably already got a clump growing next to the compost heap or at the base of the hedge. Just let them be but keep an eye on them and only dig out a few roots when they threaten to spill over into other areas of the garden.

Many butterflies have caterpillars that feed on wild grasses – including small skippers, walls, marbled whites and ringlets – so another easy way to entice them into your garden is to leave a patch of lawn unmown. There's even a caterpillar that will eat that dreaded garden weed couch grass – the larva of the speckled wood.

Some shrubs are caterpillar food plants too, such as buckthorn (*Rhamnus cathartica*) for brimstones and holly (*Ilex* spp.) for holly blues. Willows are one of the food plants of the spectacular hawkmoth caterpillars.

right No one's actually asking you to go out and plant nettles, but if you already have a clump, leave it in place – nettles are the food plant of several species of butterfly larvae.

Birdseed plants

Rigorous cutting regimes for roadside shoulders can lead to local shortages of seed-bearing plants. A few strategic species in your garden will benefit seed-eating birds.

WILDFLOWERS

It's hard to decide how to classify the teasel. It is a spectacularly useful all-round wildlife-friendly plant, and a useful illustration of a seed-bearing plant that birds like. Its egg-shaped flower heads literally bristle with seeds in autumn and are a favourite with various finches and sparrows. But before that the flowers themselves are a valuable nectar source for bees and butterflies. Insects and birds will also drink from pools of rain or dew that collect in the deep pockets formed where the leaves meet the stem.

Teasels are strong, rugged plants, more than capable of supporting a flock of feeding goldfinches. So are sunflowers, their seedheads a veritable honeycomb of tightly packed seeds that can be left to mature on the plant or cut off and hung from a bird table or tree. Many plants, however, are far too fragile to take the weight of even one passing sparrow. It's amazing how far a bird will go to take advantage of an interesting food source. Some seed-eating birds will do a clumsy imitation of a hummingbird to get at the seeds of plants too delicate to take their weight. Bullfinches are fond of the seeds of hardy geraniums and hover briefly to get at the seed pods.

CULTIVATED FLOWERS

Other seed plants include golden rod (*Solidago* spp.), Michaelmas daisies and evening primrose (*Oenothera biennis*), which are good nectar plants too.

The current trend for growing ornamental grasses in the garden has got to be good for birds. Although many of these species are not native, especially the giant grasses, they produce the sort of seed that birds love. Already gardeners are starting to notice that birds will strip the seed from grasses like *Stipa* – it's taken them a while to recognize them as a food plant but now they're getting the message.

WEEDS

Weeds, or plants perhaps better described as the less attractive species of wildflowers, are nevertheless highly attractive to garden birds. Chickweed (*Stellaria media*) is one of the more tolerable garden weeds – not as invasive as dock and far easier to pull out than bindweed – and it is worth putting up with the odd patch on bare ground. It is a good food source for seed-eaters like sparrows, which eat both ripe and unripe seed. (Anyone who has kept a budgie or canary will already know all about chickweed, as a handful is considered a treat for cage birds.) The same is true of groundsel and it too is a relatively controllable weed/wildflower.

Thistles produce masses of soft, downy seed popular with goldfinches, and there are several species of wild thistle that happily make the transition from being seen as a useful wildlife plant to a downright desirable garden plant (see Biennials, page 152).

Cow parsley (*Anthriscus sylvestris*) is increasingly appearing in the hedgerows and borders of more experimental gardeners who like its open, lacy appearance as a backdrop to flowers such as tulips and bluebells, as well as being grown in wildlife-friendly gardens. This is very good news for birds such as greenfinches, which eat its seeds.

above left Golden rod (*Solidago* spp.) is easy to grow and spreads readily by self-seeding – it's the plant's prolific seed production that attracts small birds.

below left Michaelmas daisies produce plenty of seed after flowering in autumn.

right Dried stems of teasel – the bristly seedheads are a favourite of seed-eaters like sparrows and goldfinches.

Early-flowering plants

The first spring-flowering bulbs and plants are a lifeline for overwintering insects in search of nectar after a long period of dormancy.

Many species of butterfly overwinter as adults, tucked into crevices in dry-stone walls, in sheds and in thick hedges. It's surprising how a few hours of sunshine can rouse these and other hibernating insects on the most unpromising winter's day and, if they are to have a chance of survival, they need to find an early source of nectar.

CULTIVATED PLANTS

Even in winter you can rely on a few early-flowering plants to help out. Bees appreciate early yellow crocuses – although butterflies may have difficulty reaching the nectar source – and primroses. (You may have noticed that sparrows attack yellow crocuses – it is thought they do so to get at the protein-rich pollen.)

Following on from crocuses are grape hyacinths, which have the sort of flower head that butterflies prefer – masses of small blue flowers packed tightly together in a single head. Then come purple honesty flowers, pale mauve and white sweet rocket, and aubrieta in shades of purple and pink that vary in intensity. Caterpillars such as those of the orange-tip butterfly, that feed on garlic mustard in the wild, will also feed on the leaves of both honesty and sweet rocket, saving your garden from the invasive clutches of garlic mustard.

The flowers of crown imperials produce huge drops of nectar at the base of each flower, which you can see if you lift a drooping flower head towards you. The droplets are so large that it is thought that they may even appeal to small birds such as bluetits.

WEEDS

Another surprising source of early nectar is the dandelion – not the most popular garden plant but a wildflower that is worth putting up with at this bleak time of year, even if you do pull it up later when the garden is in full bloom. (Even if you root out every visible dandelion plant, you needn't worry about a shortage for next spring as it is an efficient self-seeder.)

above   Spring-flowering crocuses are popular with bees and sparrows.

Late-flowering plants

Insects on the wing until winter need a last-minute nectar supply before hibernating, and there's a range of flowers that can help.

Just as early-flowering plants are important to insects waking from a long winter's sleep, so late-flowering plants have a vital role to play in boosting their food reserves before winter sets in.

Ivy is one of the most important late-flowering species, its curious blooms attract a whole range of late-flying bees, wasps, butterflies and other insects as it comes into flower in autumn and carries on well into winter. The berries that follow are popular with birds.

Michaelmas daisies and ice plants (*Sedum spectabile*) have nectar-rich flowers that carry on blooming until the first frosts, as do lavender and red valerian. Again with Michaelmas daisies, look for the original species, which will have the most nectar and will also produce a good crop of seeds to attract small seed-eating finches and other birds.

Winter-flowering shrubs like *Viburnum bodnantense*, witch hazel (*Hamamelis* spp.) and cherry (*Prunus* x *subhirtella)*, provide nectar even in the coldest weather, as does the winter-flowering clematis species *C. armandii*, which has strongly scented, greeny-white flowers. It is also evergreen and, as it is a vigorous climber under the right conditions, it also provides a good nesting and roosting site.

above right   Ice plants (*Sedum spectabile*) are one of the latest-flowering plants and have the sort of flower heads that insects love – flat and packed with individual florets.

below right   Michaelmas daisies flower on until the first frosts in spectacular bursts of colour, from pink to purple to cerise.

Getting the balance right

For years we've been encouraged to run our gardens like a well-organized household with the emphasis on neatness and tidiness. Now we need to think again.

Plants that didn't perform to perfection used to be frowned upon and any evidence that creatures lived in the garden – the odd nibbled leaf, the less than perfect petal – were seen as evidence that we were failing as gardeners. But a garden is a living, breathing microcosm, a balancing act between hundreds of species of plant, insect, bird and animal. The minute we start being overly tidy, fretting about insect pests to the extent of using chemicals to control them, we throw the whole garden out of balance.

By keeping the ecobalance of your garden firmly in mind, you'll be working with nature and not against it. Leaving wild corners and undisturbed areas will mean that useful predators like toads and frogs will hang around long enough to make an impression on the slug population.

Creating a wildlife-friendly garden means that you need to develop a whole new attitude towards garden maintenance. Traditional seasonal tasks, like the great autumn tidy-up, for example, are positively counterproductive in trying to establish a thriving garden ecosystem. In cities and towns, allotments are valuable wildlife oases, especially now many gardeners manage their plots organically.

right Don't be in a hurry to tidy up – leave the odd jumbled corner and positively welcome self-seeded plants like this giant wild mullein.

far right Compost heaps, old sheds and piles of stakes all create mini habitats on a typical allotment site.

In the borders

Put previous prejudices firmly behind you – a uniformly tidy herbaceous border is not a wildlife-friendly one.

There's absolutely no point in cutting down spent flower stems in the border. Even if birds have taken most of the seed from the seedheads, the old stems still have a role to play. Hollow stems of sunflowers and hollyhocks are ideal overwintering spots for ladybirds and other beneficial insects, so aim to leave them in place all winter if you can. If a tatty sunflower stem is becoming an eyesore, the solution is to cut it down but place it under a hedge where it can still act as a winter insect shelter.

Many winter stems can be attractive border features in their own right, especially with a light tracing of frost on a winter morning. This is particularly true of umbelliferous plants like fennel and angelica. Spent flower stems of ice plants (*Sedum spectabile*) have a similar wintry appeal, and leaving them in place also gives an extra degree of protection to the next year's stems developing at the base. Withered hydrangea flowers also play an important part in sheltering the flower buds for the next summer as well as providing hiding places for garden spiders and other insects.

right This woolly-leaved, woolly-stemmed wild mullein is a mass of stems at different stages, some in full flower and some on the point of setting seed. Resist the urge to cut it back and you'll have seedlings for next year, a supply of seed for the birds, and plenty of shelter for insects among the stems and leaves.

far right A log heap will ensure, your garden is full of many insects and other creatures which, in turn, attract other wildlife including toads, frogs and small birds.

Log heaps

Next to providing a pond, creating a log heap is probably the single best way to boost the variety and the insect population in your garden – not to mention the creatures that feed on them.

If you have an open fire you'll have noticed that it's always a good idea to brush off logs when bringing them in to burn, otherwise you risk incinerating creatures like beetles, spiders and woodlice.

Dead and decaying wood is a prime habitat for creepy-crawlies and their predators, so instead of bringing them indoors with every basket of logs, find a corner of the garden where you can create a permanent log heap – the base of a hedge, next to the compost heap or tucked down the side of the shed. These sites are also ideally shady, to keep the logpile cool and damp.

Many beetle grubs live in decaying wood before they turn into adults and there are even some wood-eating caterpillars, such as the larva of the goat moth. Woodlice love logs, as do centipedes and all sorts of small wasps and flies, not to mention slugs and snails. These in turn attract predators like toads and frogs, hedgehogs and field mice, and small birds such as wrens.

The damp underside of the logs is popular with juvenile newts after they have left the pond.

Use a variety of logs to construct your heap, such as oak, ash and beech. The logs should still have their bark on for insects that live in this outer layer. Adding some leaf mould or leaf litter will make the site even more attractive to toads, and a suitable place for frogs to hibernate. Hedgehogs may use a logpile for hibernating too.

Even a simple log edging for a border or raised bed increases the available habitat for wildlife and will attract insects such as wood-boring wasps, woodlice and ground beetles. But you can't take the easy way out and use ready-made log-roll edging from the garden centre as this will have been pre-treated with chemicals to stop the wood rotting by the very processes that you are trying to encourage. Instead go for the rustic look and saw down small logs of roughly the same diameter to edge your flowerbed.

Rock heaps

Rocks can be used to a similar effect as logs. The cool surface next to the soil will be home to newts and beetles, while surfaces that bake in the sun will attract lizards, slow worms and snakes.

Making a rock heap can be a useful way of dealing with builders, rubble left behind in a garden. You may need to invest in a few good-looking stones for the surface slopes but, by creating planting pockets in the heap and adding ferns and woodland plants, you can create a rockery reinvented for a shady, wild corner of the garden.

Try your hand at crude dry-stone walling with rocks, a method that relies on weight and shape to hold the wall together – no wildlife-unfriendly mortar or cement filling up all the gaps. The resulting crevices and holes make an ideal habitat for small creatures.

Try using irregular rocks to build a raised bed or a retaining wall at the edge of a terrace or slope, and complement it with trailing plants that like dry, rocky soil – aubrieta, for example, and snow-in-summer (*Cerastium tomentosum*), which will make a curtain of foliage to shelter spiders and insects.

In a big garden, instead of a rock heap you could even get away with laying a sheet of corrugated iron in a sunny spot in a rough, uncut meadow area, or somewhere out of sight of the house – it heats up quicker than rock and provides an ideal basking spot for lizards and a home for slow worms below.

right A dry-stone wall makes a perfect habitat for everything from beetles to toads to lizards, which can all find a crevice to shelter in.

Prunings and weedings

Recycling is a good idea in the garden, turning waste plant material into useful material such as compost, leaf mould and pea sticks.

Try to get out of the habit of bagging up garden waste for the dump. With a bit of lateral thinking and some careful sorting, you can deal with garden waste in a much more constructive way. Even in a small garden you can redistribute a surprising quantity of pruning material by tucking it under the hedge base for hibernating sites, or for birds and creatures to take away as nesting materials. More traditionally, you can recycle suitable twiggy branches by using them as informal stakes – pea sticks – for floppy border plants. If you are planning a mass pruning session in the garden, then consider hiring a shredder for the day – that way you can turn waste woody stems into a useful mulch (see page 100).

Most weeds can go on the compost heap to add to the pile of rotting material. The exceptions to watch out for are pernicious perennial weeds such as ground elder and dock, which can form new plants from small pieces of root. To sap every bit of vitality from these ruthless invaders, try soaking them in water before tying them up in a black plastic sack. After a few months of this treatment it should be safe to add them to the compost heap.

above left Most spent plant material can go straight on the compost heap unless it contains perennial weeds.

below left Rake up autumn leaves and compost them in a separate heap to produce a crumbly leaf mould to enrich soil or use as a mulch.

Beneficial garden insects

By boosting the habitat for predatory insects, you will find that you have less of a problem with the troublesome garden pests that they prey on.

APHIDS

Ladybirds and their larvae are voracious feeders on aphids. Making sure adults can overwinter safely (see page 36), is one positive step you can take. The next one is to leave a patch of nettles in the garden. As the first shoots emerge in early spring they are colonized by an early species of aphid that plays a vital role in the ladybird diet until the mass invasion of your roses later on in the season.

Other aphid-feeders include hoverflies – each larva will eat several hundred aphids before it turns into an adult. Adult hoverflies can be tempted into the garden to breed by growing the right sort of nectar-producing flowers (see page 28).

Lacewing larvae eat aphids too and the best way of boosting the lacewing population in your garden is to ensure that the adults have somewhere to overwinter (see page 109).

left   Like bees, wasps and hornets are pollinators too, as well as efficient disposers of dead and decaying material.

above   Ladybirds are efficient aphid-killers.

WASPS AND BEES

Despite their habit of plaguing humans during summer lunches on the terrace, it may surprise you to discover that wasps are actually on your side when it comes to gardening. They can make serious inroads into cabbage-white caterpillar populations in the vegetable garden, leaving some brassicas for you to harvest. They also efficiently deal with houseflies and with dead and decaying animal remains in the garden. As a wasps' nest is used for just a year – the whole colony dies out in winter, apart from the queen – it really is best to try and put up with it, unless it is in a very awkward position such as next to the back door or close to a window.

Bees need no introduction. Garden plants would produce no fruit or seed if bees weren't around to play their vital role in pollinating flowers. Unlike honeybees kept by beekeepers, many garden bees lead a fairly solitary life, with each female making its own small nest. Mason bees use small holes in brick and stone work; leafcutter bees may make use of a hollow plant stem or holes bored in dead wood by a beetle, and make the nest cells with neatly cut semicircles of leaf, typically rose leaves.

Bumblebees make larger nests, perhaps in a disused mousehole, and build up a small colony over the summer; even so, the colony will be nowhere near the size of a honeybee colony, as bumblebee colonies die out at the end of the year whereas honeybees overwinter in the hive.

By forgoing pesticides and herbicides and by being a bit more relaxed about garden tidiness, you can assure the survival of beneficial insects.

Natural nesting sites

Creating nest sites for birds in your garden is an important way of redressing the balance that has been upset by man's actions over the decades.

As the management of the countryside has changed over the years, there has been a very real loss of nesting habitat for birds. Where farming has become more and more mechanized and tractors and combine harvesters ever larger and more sophisticated, so fields have been merged and made bigger by the grubbing-out of hedgerows, with the loss of miles of natural nesting sites. Even farm buildings have changed so that modern barns are soulless metal bunkers, and tumbledown barns, where owls and swallows can nest, are an increasing rarity. Old barns are in demand for conversion to human homes, with a loss of habitat for birds. There's pressure from all sides – even in gardens there's the urge to use every inch of space, to tidy up every corner, pull out every wildflower. In the wildlife-friendly garden you can redress the balance in a number of ways.

Putting up nest boxes is one answer (see Net Boxes for Birds, page 64) but these will attract birds that typically nest in holes or crevices in trees and walls. Birds that nest 'in the open' have a harder time of things.

right Rambling or climbing roses make good nesting sites, offering plenty of cover and extra protection if thorny.

far right Thick, dense hedges offer nesting birds shelter and protection. Avoid pruning from early spring until early autumn and you won't risk disturbing nests.

CLIMBERS

Introducing climbing plants into a garden is one of the most important things you can do to provide nesting sites, whether you use them to cover a garden shed, a fence or wall, or even a house wall.

Ivy

One of the best and easiest climbers to grow is ivy. Many householders have tended to avoid growing ivy on the walls of the house as it has a reputation for damaging brickwork, but it is really only a problem if its tendrils get under roof tiles or hanging vertical tiles. For birds, ivy has everything to commend it:

- it is evergreen so provides year-round shelter;
- it forms stout stems that can easily support nests;
- it harbours insects for insectivorous birds;
- its berries are a food source for many bird species.

But there's no need to have ivy against the house – it can do its job just as well growing up a fence, over a shed or (perhaps best of all) over a dead or dying tree. Wherever you choose to plant it, set the new ivy plant at least 30cm (1ft) away from the vertical surface it is to cover, so that the roots have the best chance of benefiting from rainfall. Then ruthlessly cut it back to a few centimetres (inches) tall, to stimulate lots of new shoots. As these appear, just guide them towards the wall or fence with a cane or two; once the ivy hits the vertical surface it will do the rest itself by means of aerial roots – no wires or trellis required.

Honeysuckle

Honeysuckle is another invaluable wild climber that grows thickly with a good tangle of stems that make natural nesting sites, but this is a climber that needs help to scale the heights. On a wall, the best thing you can do is to nail battens to the wall and then attach pieces of trellis to the battens. This creates an ideal cavity between the curtain of honeysuckle and the wall, where birds can nest, and the battens make good ledges that the birds can build up into nest sites. As before, set new plants away from the base of the wall where rain is less likely to penetrate and then train new growth back towards the wall along canes set at an angle.

Clematis

Mature clematis plants grow stout-enough stems and are densely tangled enough to support and conceal birds' nests. And, in a garden with no obvious vertical sites, they can be trained over an archway or pergola specifically to create a natural nesting site. For a pergola or arch, choose one of the less vigorous species: old favourites like 'Nelly Moser' and the 'Jackmanii' varieties have big summer flowers and thicken up nicely without swamping the entire structure. Rampant clematis such as spring-flowering *Clematis montana* need more space: use it to cover a bare fence or to conceal an ugly shed, or grow it through an old tree that is on its last legs. An apple tree that is no longer productive can become an ideal nesting site by letting a clematis scramble through its branches, providing cover and protection for birds and their nestlings.

Hedges

Planting a hedge is an excellent garden bird habitat booster and will make a real difference in terms of food, shelter and nesting site. (For instructions see page 88.) In bird-friendly terms a hedge needs to be thick, dense and twiggy. It should be at least 2m (6½ft) high and 1m (3ft) wide if possible. Evergreen bushes have the advantage of providing permanent leaf cover and shelter but many deciduous shrubs come into leaf early enough to shield new nests.

In country gardens, mixed hedges of native species blend in well and mimic the loss of natural hawthorn and hazel hedges.

Planting a hedge from scratch means that it will take 2–3 years before it starts to contribute to the habitat, but you can see if adding annual climbers helps attract nesting birds. If the embryonic hedge is reinforced by a boundary marker such as chicken wire or chain mail, it won't hamper the bushes' development if you add a quick-growing annual or two to make a bit of cover. Nasturtiums, the cup and saucer vine, and the Chilean glory vine all make massive amounts of growth that might tempt a bird to nest, and they can be used against a wall or fence while you are establishing a more permanent climber.

In a suburban garden you may already have a hedge of flowering shrubs like forsythia, flowering currant and viburnum, which is a valuable nesting habitat. Even the much-maligned *Cupressocyparis leylandii* is a favourite nesting place for blackbirds and thrushes, despite being a non-native species.

above Training a climber along the eaves of a shed is a neat way to create an extra habitat without losing space in the garden. This passionflower will also attract bees, butterflies and other insects.

right Ivy is one of the best climbers for nesting birds. Its stout stems provide nesting ledges and its evergreen leaves give shelter from sun and rain.

left Sparrows and other small birds strip the soft fluffy seedheads of pampas grass (*Cortaderia selloana*) to line their nests.

Just add water

Water is perhaps the single most important element that will transform a garden into a mini nature reserve.

All creatures need water to drink and, whilst insects and small birds can make use of dewdrops or raindrops on vegetation, the permanence of a pond or bird bath will make a big difference to the creatures that visit a garden.

BIRD BATHS

Garden centres sell all sorts of gorgeous and elaborate bird baths, but the birds themselves will be quite happy bathing in and drinking from an old baking tin or an inverted dustbin lid set on a couple of bricks on the lawn. The most important factor about a bird bath is depth: 7.5cm (3in) is perfect. Its sides should slope gradually and should not be slippery. If you have a glazed terracotta bird bath, a layer of gravel will make it more user-friendly for the birds and you can also use gravel to raise the base of a bird bath that may be too deep.

Shallow water warms up quickly, which is ideal for birds bathing in winter, but in summer it will mean that the bird bath needs topping up daily. You can also get algal growth in bird baths and the water does tend to go stagnant, so regular scrubbing out and refilling is a good idea.

Birds need to bathe, even in winter, to keep their plumage in good shape. When other water sources are frozen, you can make sure a bird bath has an ice-free area by floating a ping-pong ball on the surface. Freezing ice can't get to grips with the ball's surface.

A bird bath should be out in the open so that birds can keep a lookout for predators such as cats. In neighbourhoods with a high population of cats, it is worth investing in a hanging bird bath that swings freely from a chain or one that is at least 1.5m (5ft) high, typically an iron pole with a support that encircles a concrete or terracotta bowl.

PONDS

No garden is too small to have a pond and almost nothing is too small to serve as a pond. Even on a balcony or terrace it is still possible to grow a water lily in a glazed pot. Where there is space for a border or lawn, instead of using a dustbin lid as a bird bath, you can turn it into a pond by sinking it into the ground and adding a few small rocks and water plants. You'll be amazed at the variety of life that will thrive in a pond that size: caddis fly larvae, freshwater shrimps, water fleas, water snails and pond-skaters may all make their home there.

By upping the stakes just a little you can add a whole lot more. A small pond not more than 1m (3ft) in diameter will attract birds to drink and bathe. Amphibians must have water to breed and so frogs, toads and newts that have been hibernating under logs and rocks will use the pond to mate and produce spawn.

Many insects have an underwater larval stage and the insect populations that a small pond supports will be enough to attract insectivorous birds such as swallows and house martins swooping low over the water. And once dusk has fallen their place will be taken by bats after the same prey.

above right This densely planted pond provides cover for small creatures, such as frogs and toads, entering and leaving the water. The planting includes candelabra primula, astilbe, and lady's mantle.

below right Yellow flag or yellow water iris, is an imported relative of the native blue flag and looks just as good in garden pools.

left This bird bath is perfectly sited with clear all-around access and a nearby tall vantage point – the rose-covered pergola – for birds to sit and wait their turn.

Containers as ponds

All sorts of containers can be recycled and take on a new life as a garden pond: old stone cattle troughs, stone sinks, butler sinks and classroom sinks can be made watertight and planted up. However, although an old butler sink with its plughole blocked is better than no pond at all, what it lacks is a shallow end and it should have an island of rocks, at the very least, to attract perching birds or to help creatures climb out. Drowning isn't just an issue with small children – birds and mammals can drown too if they cannot easily scramble out of the water, while froglets and young newts can find themselves similarly trapped.

Safety first

Ideally every pond should have a shallow end rather like a beach where the pond bed gradually shelves down into deeper water. This allows birds to use the pond for drinking and bathing, small mammals like hedgehogs to drink safely at the water's edge, and all sorts of other creatures to come and go. (For full instructions on making a pond, see page 75.)

To make a pond safe for children, one of the neatest ideas is to add a strong metal grid more or less level with the surface of the water. The grid should be large enough to go right over the pond so that the edging slabs (or turf) will sit on top of it and hold it in place. The grid's mesh can be wide enough to allow frogs to pass through and water plants to grow up, without compromising child safety. As well as making the pond safe for children it means they can still enjoy it too – fencing a pond off, for example, only makes it more tempting.

Bog gardens

Adding a bog garden to one side of a pond also increases the available wildlife habitat. By running

the pond liner under the soil for a foot or more, any plants grown there will be able to draw water directly from the pond. The damp, muddy soil will also be appreciated by blackbirds, who use mud to line their nests, and by swallows and martins, whose nests are

constructed almost entirely from beakfuls of mud. In dry weather in spring, it can be a good idea to use a watering can or two of water to make a muddy puddle if you know you have swallows or martins nesting nearby.

above An ambitious water feature in a large garden can include running water as well as still; here a rocky miniature waterfall is flanked by yellow monkey flower (*Mimulus*), and ferns.

Making wildlife feel at home

Loss of habitat, and particularly of nesting sites, means that many wild creatures are essentially homeless. By putting up nesting boxes or bat boxes, you can make a big difference to breeding success rates. In this chapter you'll discover which nest boxes appeal to which species, and small changes, to your garden that will make a big difference to breeding birds. Feeding birds, too (and not just in winter), can make a dramatic difference to the populations in your garden.

Bird feeders and tables

Birds don't just need help with breeding sites. In an environment that has increasingly been manipulated by insecticides and herbicides, food can be scarce too.

By setting up a bird table or bird feeder in your garden, you can improve the survival rate of small birds over the winter. Birds are your allies in the garden, feeding (depending on the species) on slugs, snails, aphids and other insect pests. So it makes good gardening sense to encourage them into your backyard. Supplementing their diet with nuts and seeds in winter, when wild foods are in short supply, will stand you in good stead later in the season when the first insect pests start to appear.

Once you've started feeding the birds, you're committed. Forgetting to put food out when birds have made visiting your feeding table part of their daily routine can jeopardize their survival, especially in severe winter weather.

above Make your own fat balls by using melted lard or suet to bind together a mixture of birdseed, peanuts, oats, raisins, currants or sultanas, grated cheese and cake crumbs (more nutritious than breadcrumbs). As a rough guide, use about one-third fat to two-thirds of dry mixture.

right A free-standing bird table out in the open allows birds to feed with minimal risk from ground-based predators like cats.

far right A rustic hanging feeder provides a safe feeding place.

What to feed birds

Probably the best, easiest and cheapest way to feed garden birds is to bulk-buy seeds and nuts from a specialist birdfood company, and then supplement these with suitable kitchen scraps. Investing in a big storage tub and a seed scoop for filling bird feeders makes the whole process neater and more efficient.

Small birds weighing in at anything between ½oz and 1oz (10–30g) need to eat 40% of their body weight every day in severe weather and, as they have no fat reserves, they need a high-energy diet.

Peanuts

Peanuts are the traditional, familiar birdfood put out for tits and finches. Quality is all-important: by feeding poor-grade nuts you can actually do more harm than good. Cheap nuts are prone to a fungal infection that produces aflatoxin, which is poisonous to birds. It's best to buy from a specialist birdfood company that can guarantee its stocks are aflatoxin-free. Storing peanuts carelessly can also increase the risk of aflatoxin production. Always keep them in an airtight container in a cool, dry cupboard or shed.

Sunflower seeds

Research – and observation by gardeners – has shown that many birds actually prefer sunflower seeds to peanuts. Two types are generally on sale, black and striped: the black ones have a higher oil content and so it's not surprising that birds tend to go for these first.

Sunflower seeds can be slightly more expensive to buy than peanuts, so you may like to put out a mixture of the two. They are also more messy to feed, as the birds eat only the inner seed and the discarded hulls can soon build up. If you don't want the discipline of sweeping them up regularly, you can buy ready-hulled seeds, sometimes sold as sunflower hearts.

Seed mixes

To attract a wide range of seed-eating birds, look out for special 'wild bird' seed mixes. These may contain any or all of the following: sunflower seeds (both black and striped), kibbled maize, millet, chopped peanuts, corn, oatmeal and canary seed.

Live food

Really dedicated wildlife gardeners know that the breeding season is a critical feeding time for birds. Many small birds feed their young on insects and, in years where bad spring weather has led to a shortage of caterpillars and other grubs, fewer nestlings survive. Now it is possible to improve their chances by putting out 'live foods'. Specialist birdfood companies offer plastic tubs packed with mealworms or waxworms, which are ideal foods for robins, blackbirds, wrens, thrushes and starlings. The main snag with feeding mealworms is that, if you order a large quantity, you'll have to start feeding the mealworms themselves before you feed them to the birds!

If you really can't face dipping into a tub of squirming worms, look out for dried mealworms, which are said to be just as nutritious.

KITCHEN SCRAPS

We've been feeding birds stale bread for years, but there has always been some doubt as to how nutritious it is. Current thinking in the bird world states that bread is all right providing it is moist – dry bread can swell inside the bird's crop or stomach, with the risk of choking it. Soaking bread slices in water before squeezing them out and crumbling them is one solution; mixing breadcrumbs with dripping or bacon fat from the frying pan makes them even more appetizing to birds.

Other suitable crumbly scraps include stale cake crumbs and biscuit crumbs. Try putting out leftover mashed potato or even the skins of potatoes baked in their jackets – there's usually enough flesh left for the birds to pick over.

Suet figures frequently when the feeding of birds is discussed but, unless you are a committed dumpling-maker or steamed pudding fanatic, suet doesn't tend to be a kitchen cupboard staple. If you are lucky enough to have a proper butcher's shop nearby, then this is probably the easiest place to buy suet specially for the birds: buy it in bulk, chop it up and freeze it in useful portions.

right   For a rustic, natural look, make a log feeder by drilling holes in the top of a log to hold seeds and nuts. Attach a length of chain using U-shaped staples and hang it on a tree.

Bird tables

Putting out food on a proper bird table lets birds feed in relative safety and gives them a fixed feeding station to visit each day.

Bird tables can be as elaborate or as simple as you like. At the top end of the scale are tables with shingle roofs and integral feeders and water dishes. At the opposite extreme, a simple pole-mounted tray is just as efficient. It's just a question of style and what suits your garden environment.

An old wooden fruit tray can be reused as a bird table by mounting it on its own post or on a sturdy section of fence or gatepost. Its raised sides are ideal for preventing food being blown away. An old bun tray makes an instant bird table with individual compartments for different foods – just nail it to a simple garden stake.

All tables should be between 1.5–2m (5–6½ft) above ground to keep birds safe from cats and other predators. Siting a table in an open spot gives you a good view of feeding birds as well as allowing them all-round vision, but don't site it too far from perching points such as trees and bushes.

If you're making a table from new wood, always choose untreated timber to avoid introducing harmful chemicals into the garden. Many tables now have a fine metal mesh base that lets rainwater drain away and so stops food spoiling so quickly in wet weather – it's a design worth copying.

To stop squirrels using a pole-mounted bird table, pass the pole through an inverted biscuit tin just below the table – this stops squirrels climbing straight up. Smearing the pole with petroleum jelly is also said to deter squirrels from climbing and will put off cats too.

Don't forget ground-feeding birds. Blackbirds, thrushes, robins and wrens tend to prefer to feed at ground level rather than visit a table. Any wrinkled or soft fruit from the fruit bowl can go straight out for the blackbirds – they seem to prize pears especially. Grated cheese scattered at the base of a hedge will fortify robins and wrens on frosty days.

WHAT TO FEED BIRDS

In addition to proper birdfoods, add small quantities of table scraps such as:

- breadcrumbs
- fruit peelings and scraps
- cooked potato
- dried fruits
- cooked rice (no salt)
- oats
- grated cheese
- grated suet

WHAT NOT TO FEED BIRDS

Do not include:

- salty foods such as salted peanuts or crisps
- uncooked rice
- desiccated coconut
- dried peas, beans, lentils (as many small birds cannot digest these)

above   Recycle an old bun or baking tin by nailing it to a secure post or stake for an instant bird table.

left   Old apple boxes make good bird-table tops – their raised sides stop seed and other lightweight foods from being blown away. Drill drainage holes in a couple of corners so that rainwater will trickle away before it spoils food.

How to feed birds

Matching the right container to the right birdfood can spell the difference between disaster and success – there's nothing more frustrating than seeing the contents of a feeder spilled across the ground minutes after you've filled it.

Threading peanuts (sold in their shells) onto lengths of string can keep children quiet for half an hour. Give them a blunt darning needle threaded with gardening twine and show them how to knot the twine round the first nut to hold the rest in place. As it takes birds longer to extract the nuts from a shell than from a feeder, the benefit of this method is that you get more time to watch the birds in your garden.

For ready-shelled peanuts, the simplest feeders are plastic mesh cylinders but, where squirrels visit a garden to compete for food, these designs don't stand a chance against a squirrel's strong teeth. (Nylon mesh bags are no longer recommended for feeding as birds can become trapped in the fabric.) Tough metal feeders will last longer and there are various extra squirrel-proofing measures that have been developed, including cages or guards that fit over a central cylinder, with bars too narrow to admit a squirrel. If you use one of these, be patient. It may take several days before the birds themselves feel comfortable about using a cage-style feeder.

Birdseed feeders are similar in design but the seed-holding cylinder is usually made of tough plastic with feeding holes and perches at intervals.

Always hang feeders out of reach of cats. Hanging them from a chain or rod, so that they swing freely, also deters larger, clumsier birds from monopolizing the feeder.

When to feed birds

Children and dogs like routine, and it seems that birds do too. Do try to stick to regular feeding times when at all possible – incorporating the filling up of the bird feeder as part of your own breakfast-time routine is one way of ensuring that you don't forget to feed the birds.

In winter try to feed birds twice a day. The critical times are first thing in the morning when birds need to boost energy lost keeping warm on cold nights, and then again just before it gets dark, to top up their energy levels for the coming night.

Although you want birds to tackle insect pests in summer, they will still appreciate a range of foods being set out. Feeding nestlings is hard work and adult birds can do with a bit of help. Current thinking is that peanuts should not be placed loose on a bird table in summer as they are not suitable for nestlings – you can, however, continue to offer peanuts in a mesh feeder that doesn't allow the birds to remove a whole nut, or you can buy chopped peanuts instead. Many adult birds moult in summer and feeding them high-protein foods such as black sunflower seeds, grated cheese and oats will help this process.

left If you're feeling creative, make your own decorative bird feeders like these grass seedhead wreaths on an old shed door. Clockwise from top left, the different grasses are fox-tail millet; a mixture of brome and millet; fox-tail millet; and quaking grass.

right Make a decorative wreath to feed the birds by wiring dried sunflower heads and poppy heads to a stout wire circle, along with grasses such as fox-tail millet, wheat, oats and quaking grass. Buy the grasses from petfood shops or dry them yourself – avoid any that may have been sprayed with pesticides. See page 60 for more ideas.

Making your own bird feeders

Bird feeders needn't be shop bought. With a little imagination all sorts of containers can be re-used or feeders can be made from foodstuffs themselves.

Fresh coconuts have long been popular bird treats. Use a handsaw to cut the coconut in half. This job is best done outside in case the coconut still has 'milk' inside. Then use the saw to cut three grooves in each half-shell to hold string in place for hanging. Knot three lengths of string together and position the knot under the shell, then hang it on a tree or bush (see picture on page 53). There's no reason why you shouldn't add a handful of sunflower seeds or peanuts to attract birds to the coconut. Then when the bluetits have pecked every last scrap of nut flesh from the empty shell, it can be used to hold a handful of seeds or nuts, or refilled with a mixture of fat and oats (see recipe opposite).

Many birdseed mixes contain millet, oats, corn and sunflower seeds. You can take these back a step and weave together sprays of millet and oats, stems of corn and dried sunflower seedheads to make a decorative wreath to feed seed-eating birds. For the most natural effect, pliable stems of clematis or honeysuckle make a good wreath base, but gardener's wire will do the job too. Then just tuck in stems of your chosen seed-bearing grasses. Hang the wreath against a tree trunk or on the side of a shed – it won't be sturdy enough to allow to swing freely.

HOMEMADE FAT BALLS

1. Make your own fat balls by using melted lard or suet to bind together a mixture of birdseed, peanuts, oats, raisins, currants or sultanas, grated cheese and cake crumbs (more nutritious than breadcrumbs). As a rough guide, use about one-third fat to two-thirds of dry mixture.

2. Press the mixture into an empty half-coconut or a purpose-designed clay 'bell', or thread a length of twine through an old plastic cup or yogurt pot and hold it taut centrally while you press in the mixture.

3. Tie a matchstick to one end of the twine to stop the fat ball slipping off when unmoulded, and hang the finished fat ball in a tree or bush.

4. You can also press the fat-ball mixture into decaying logs and then place these in the garden where tree-feeding birds such as woodpeckers and treecreepers can find them.

left   Half a coconut is a valuable birdfood in itself but can also act as a container for striped sunflower seeds. The sunflower seeds will also attract birds that don't necessarily recognize the unfamiliar.

right   A selection of home-made fat balls, nut garlands and pine cone feeders hung in a garden tree will attract small birds – for 'recipe' instructions see page 61.

BIRDFOOD RECIPES

Pine cone feeders

1. Collect a handful of pine cones – large ones will be easiest to use – and knot a length of string tightly around each one, tying it between the scales near the top of the cone. (Shake the pine cone over a sheet of newspaper first and catch any pine nuts that are left and add these to the mixture too.)

2. Melt a 500g (1lb) block of lard in a saucepan over a gentle heat. Take it off the stove and stir in 250g (8oz) of oatmeal or porridge oats.

3. Once the mixture is cool enough to handle, but not set hard, roll each pinecone in it, then press and shape it with your hands.

4. Hang up the cones indoors to harden before stringing them up for the birds. Prepared pine cone feeders can be stored in the fridge for a week or so.

Nut and berry garland

1. Thread a darning needle with gardening twine and push it through an unshelled peanut and knot the end.

2. Continue threading on a mixture of peanuts, dried apricots, raisins, walnut halves, crab apples, rosehips, hawthorn berries or any garden berries you have to hand.

3. Once you have a garland about 30cm (1ft) long, hang it from a tree or bush, out of reach of cats.

Keeping tables and feeders clean

The following guidelines should ensure that your bird tables and feeders remain in tip-top condition throughout the year.

• Keep an eye on your bird table and note which foods hang around for longest and are therefore more likely to spoil. Then you can feed according to the birds' needs and reduce waste.

• Try to scrub solid bird tables as soon as they begin to look unattractive. Do this outside using hot water and a scrubbing brush kept specially for the purpose. You can add a very small quantity of disinfectant to the water, but then it is very important to rinse away all traces afterwards – the birdfood supplier that you use may also stock specially formulated cleansers that are harmless to birds and wildlife.

• Metal mesh tables are far easier to clean – just tip away surplus food and scrub thoroughly. Wash out nut feeders regularly – putting your thumb over the end of the garden hose to increase the water pressure can help to flush debris out of awkward corners.

• Bird tables need to be kept clean not only to avoid spreading disease amongst birds, but also to prevent any disease spreading to humans. Wear rubber gloves if possible when cleaning tables and feeders and wash your hands thoroughly afterwards; don't bring feeders into the house to clean them.

• Sweep up the area surrounding the bird table every few days or you may end up attracting rats into the garden.

• In summer, good bird-table hygiene is paramount when food is far more likely to go rotten so adjust your routine accordingly.

above Nest boxes benefit from good hygiene practices too.

right A wreath of dried grass seed is one of the cleanest and tidiest ways to feed seed-eating birds – just make sure you sweep up husks and dropped seed from time to time.

Nest boxes for birds

The increasing urbanization of the countryside, with fewer open barns and tumbledown outbuildings, and the fact that there is less wasteland in cities and towns, means the habitat for nesting birds has been drastically reduced.

Putting up a nest box or two in your garden, or a simple nest platform, can make an appreciable difference to broody birds. Don't be disappointed if a pair of robins don't move in within weeks: it can take months before a nest box is accepted – and even if birds don't nest in it, they may well use it as a roost on winter nights. Other wildlife may move in: butterflies may overwinter in an empty bird box, bats may use it, bees or wasps may nest in it or field mice may take it over. Whatever the outcome, your efforts won't have been in vain.

Basically there are two types of nest box – the fully enclosed sort with an entrance hole for access, and the open platform. Between them these two designs cater for the nesting requirements of most garden bird species. Enclosed nest boxes are ideal for birds that normally nest in holes, including tits, nuthatches and starlings.

MAKING AN ENCLOSED NEST BOX

Wood really is the best material: metal and plastic both cause condensation in cold weather. Wood that is 2cm (¾in) thick is ideal. Reclaimed timber – old floorboards for example, as they are well seasoned – is fine. A simple box shape is best: don't be tempted to add finishing touches such as a perch outside the entrance hole or even a small platform – these could have a very undesirable effect and actually help predators to gain access to the nest.

You don't have to be a skilled woodworker to make a nest box but there are several tips that will make sure your efforts last a bit longer.

• If possible, use the wood so that the grain runs vertically and encourages the rain to run off quickly.

• Recessing the floor of the box will also stop rain seeping into the end grain of the floor panel.

• Assemble the box using galvanized nails or brass screws, to avoid rusting. The box will need a removable lid so that it can be cleaned from time to time (see page 72).

• Damp and cold conditions will lower nestlings' chances of survival, so if your finished box has obvious gaps and gaping joints, use a flexible filler to block these up. The point where the lid is hinged to the box is a vulnerable entry point for rainwater, so if the lid is less than snug-fitting, add a strip of roofing felt or waterproof duct tape to protect the join.

• Conversely there is the risk of nestlings overheating at the height of summer, but this can be reduced by drilling ventilation holes. Do this using the finest drill bit you have, preferably creating holes that are narrower than the average wasp or bee, to avoid attracting them to a possible nest site. Drill the holes just below the roof and drill at an upward angle so that rain won't penetrate.

• The entrance hole similarly should be well above the base of the box to stop cats and other predators sticking in a paw and scooping up nestlings. Don't be overly concerned about the diameter of the entrance hole provided it's in the right position. While it's true that bigger birds need bigger holes and vice versa, you shouldn't be trying to encourage one species to nest at the expense of another, since nest sites are in short supply whatever the species – and if a bluetit finds the entrance hole too big for its liking it will often reduce the size by blocking it with mud and grass. Other species are equally capable of pecking at a hole to enlarge it.

For a simple set of plans, see below. All the measurements are approximate; there are no ideal dimensions, but just bear in mind that the bigger the box, the more nesting material is needed to fill it, which can pose a problem for smaller birds.

MAKING AN ENCLOSED NESTING BOX

203mm (8in)

side

254mm (10in)

side

254mm (10in)

back

203mm (8in)

front

115mm (4½in)

floor

254mm (10in)

8in (203mm)

Step 1 Divide up a piece of wood as shown to form the sides, base and roof.

roof

¾in (20mm) thick

What you need:
Piece of wood measuring approximately 1029mm x 152mm (40½in x 6in)

tape measure

pencil

drill

rubber or metal hinge

Step 2 Before assembling the box, drill a hole in the front or side of the box. This should not be less than 12.7cm (5in) from the bottom of the box and should measure approximately 5cm (2in) in diameter.

batten 102mm (4in) wide to attach to wall or tree

Step 3 Attach a hinge to the lid and drill a drainage hole at the bottom of the box before attaching it to a tree or the side of a garden shed.

drainage hole

These sizes are not exact, use them as a guide.
Ensure the inside of the box measures at least 100mm (4in) square.
A piece of rubber tyre makes a good hinge.

MAKING A PLATFORM NEST BOX

Many birds prefer to nest 'in the open' and typically chose a site in the fork of two branches, in a tangle of brambles or a ledge on a wall or fence. Robins, flycatchers, thrushes and blackbirds like this sort of site. You can increase the number of available sites by setting up some simple open nest boxes in your garden. An old wooden seed tray could be cut down to make two or three smaller platforms, which can then be securely wedged in a thick hedgerow or nailed to a fence or wall behind a curtain of ivy.

A more elaborate design could be based on the enclosed nest box (see pages 64–5) with the front panel replaced by a low piece of wood, leaving a large rectangular entrance. By incorporating a roof, this design gives more protection in less ideal sites.

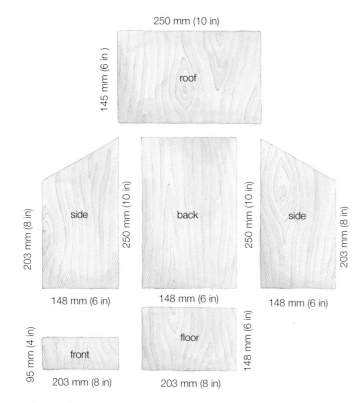

250 mm (10 in)

145 mm (6 in)

roof

203 mm (8 in)

side

250 mm (10 in)

back

250 mm (10 in)

side

203 mm (8 in)

148 mm (6 in)

148 mm (6 in)

148 mm (6 in)

95 mm (4 in)

front

148 mm (6 in)

floor

203 mm (8 in)

203 mm (8 in)

Step 1 Cut the pieces of wood from a plank of wood measuring approximately 1029 mm x 152mm (40½ in x 6 in).

Step 2 Assemble them to make the box shown, right.

left This enclosed nest box conforms to good design: the entrance hole is well above the nest-box base to prevent cats putting in a paw and scooping out nestlings; the sloping roof allows rainwater to run straight off before it can find a way into the nest box itself. A back plate helps with fixing a nest box in position, or a batten below will take any extra weight.

What you need:
Piece of wood measuring approximately 40½in x 6in (1029mm x 152mm).

tape measure

pencil

drill

This box is the same as the box shown on page 65 but it has a larger entrance to allow a greater variety of birds to use it.

NEST BUNDLES

Making a nest bundle is an ingenious way of reusing prunings from shrubs and trees. The best pruned material of all is thorny twigs from pyracantha, hawthorn, sloes or rambling roses, though you need to wear stout thorn-proof gloves to handle the stems. Gradually gather the stems into a bundle or faggot about 1m (3ft) long; you could be ambitious and make it up to 2m (6ft), but it will become more difficult to handle. Use strong garden twine to tie the bundle tightly at each end. Force open a nest cavity in the centre of the bundle and wedge it open with small struts of wood or line it with chicken wire to keep it open.

Nest bundles can be fixed to a wall or fence, or even tied to a tree trunk. Once it is in position you can make another nest site by flattening the top into a cup-shaped depression for an open nest site. Plant a clematis or honeysuckle at the base of the bundle for extra shelter and screening for nesting birds.

Step 1 Roughly trim long, twiggy prunings from garden shrubs so that they don't have too many sideshoots. Tie them into a bundle, tying firmly top and bottom with garden twine or even wire.

Step 2 Force open a space in the middle of the bundle, wedging it open with pieces of wood or chicken wire and tying the bundle into two halves.

Step 3 Hang it on a wall, fence or tree trunk, preferably sheltered by a climber to give extra protection for nesting birds.

PAPIER-MÂCHÉ CUPS

Anyone who enjoyed making papier-mâché bowls at school by gluing strips of newspaper over a balloon as a mould should have the requisite skills to make a cup-shaped nest box to attract house martins. As martins usually nest under the eaves of houses, you need to attach the cup to an L-shaped wooden frame that can be screwed to the soffits or eaves of the roof.

To make two cups, stand a football in a wide-necked jar and cover it in strips of newspaper soaked in a waterproof glue. You don't need to make a complete sphere, just cover the area sitting above the jar. Cover the football in at least three layers of paper. When it is dry, cut the papier-mâché mould in half with a sharp knife to make two cups. Use the same paper-strip-and-glue technique to attach the cup to a wooden backing board, then cut a semicircular entry hole at the top of the cup. Screw another piece of board at right angles to form the lid and use brackets or screws to attach the lid to the eaves.

Before installing the nest box you could paint it brown for authenticity, to mimic the mud more normally used by the birds themselves, finishing off with a final layer of waterproof glue.

Step 1 Make the-papier mâché cups in the traditional way, by gluing scraps of newspaper over a basketball for a mold. Stand the basketball in a wide-necked vase or jar for ease of working.

Step 2 Attach the cup to the backing board with more papier-mâché strips.

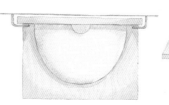

Step 3 Add a lid by screwing on another piece of wood.

Step 4 Attach the finished nesting box below the eaves of the house. Look at existing nests and choose a similar position for your artificial one.

RUSTIC LOG BOX

The quickest way to make a well-camouflaged rustic nest box is to take a log, stand it on end and split it vertically into four quarters. Then split or saw off the pointed apex of each quarter so that, when you reassemble the log, it has a hollow centre. Then you can glue it back together with waterproof glue, or simply bind it securely with wire and plug the top and bottom with chips of wood, or make a proper roof and base. A nest box like this probably won't last more than one or two seasons, but it is fun to make and easy to slot into the garden somewhere.

Keeping predators out

If you know there's likely to be a predator problem in your garden then you can take some specific steps to stop it happening again.

Tree-mounted nest boxes can be protected by tying bands of prickly prunings above and below the box – collars of gorse would be ideal; barbed wire a last resort. Smooth rubber collars, in similar positions, can break the grip of small predatory mammals such as weasels. Cats can be deterred by an additional thorny thatch of gorse or brambles tacked onto the nest-box roof.

In serious situations perhaps the best solution of all is to use hanging nest boxes – birds naturally nest in precarious sites so are not usually put off by a box that swings in the breeze. You can buy ready-made hanging nest boxes, which are usually cylindrical, suspended on strong wire that passes through an anti-predator cone to stop animals climbing down the wire. Again, try hanging home-made boxes from a length of stout chain, also protected by passing it through a cone.

WHERE TO SITE THE BOX

Siting a nest box is largely a matter of common sense and creature comforts. A box in full sunlight all day will become uncomfortably hot; in an exposed, unprotected spot it is likely to be too cold and draughty. You know your garden: choose a spot that is sheltered, partly shaded and doesn't get the full force of the wind or driving rain. Consider the flight path that birds will have to take to enter the nest: it should be free of obstructions like washing lines or garden furniture in regular use, and any bushes or shrubs that could conceal a cat in waiting. It's quite useful to have a staging post a few feet away – a branch where a parent bird can wait and survey the scene before heading into the nest box.

• Birds that nest in trees will accept a box more readily if it's hung from a tree or on a shed that is set among trees.

• Open nest platforms should be fixed to a wall with a concealing canopy of ivy or creeper, or placed in a thick hedge or even in the crook of a branch in a tree if there is dense enough leaf cover to hide it.

• Height is important from the point of view of warding off predators rather than providing any benefit to the birds – domestic cats are likely to be the commonest problem, so hang boxes at least 1.5m (5ft) up.

• Don't place a nest box too close to a bird table – the constant coming and going of feeding birds will put off potential users.

There's no particular ideal time to put up a nest box – the sooner you do it, the more time the birds have to get used to it and appraise it, and they may still use it as a roost even if it's too late in the year for breeding. If you are hanging it in early spring, a few wisps of hay in the base of the box may give any inspecting birds a hint.

above Don't worry about nailing a nest box directly to a tree – it won't do any lasting damage.

To stop sparrows, starlings and other birds from hovering under the eaves of your house and pulling out the fibreglass roof insulation, try setting out some alternative nesting materials.

• Gather things while you're out on a country walk: feathers, handfuls of hay or straw and wisps of sheep's wool snagged on barbed wire can be made into small bundles. Place some on the ground and others in trees, in the fork of a branch.

• At home, save cat and dog combings, even human hair, or scraps of wool from the knitting basket.

• Some birds like to strip twisted lengths of fibres from gnarled honeysuckle stems, or beakfuls of the soft, downy flower heads of pampas grass, to line their nests.

Making a bat box

Bats are even harder pushed to find suitable roosting and breeding sites than birds.

If you have seen bats swooping low over your garden on a summer evening, then it is worth putting up one or two bat boxes. Bats roost by clinging vertically to old walls, tree trunks etc., so a bat box needs to mimic these rough surfaces. The inside walls of the box should be rough, unplaned timber – only use untreated timber, as bats are very sensitive to chemicals – or make horizontal grooves in smooth wood using a tool such as a router, or simply roughen it up with a saw.

The box should be small so that the bats can huddle together for warmth – something along the lines of a rough rectangle 15 x 10 x 10cm (6 x 4 x 4in) will be fine. Give the box a sloping roof so that rain runs off it, and a back plate that extends below the base of the box for easy access. The box entrance should be in the base of the box, and should be a slit the width of the box and about 2cm (¾in) deep (see diagram opposite).

When deciding where to place bat boxes, look for areas unobstructed by telephone wires or overhanging branches – bats like an uncluttered flight path to their roost. Choose trees near a pond or river or that form part of a thick hedge. On the other hand, tall, isolated trees also suit bats, as they are easy to approach in flight.

Hang the boxes as high as is safely possible. If you don't have tall trees use your house; bats often roost in roofs, a bat box under the eaves is ideal. Hanging several boxes on one tree or building, but at different angles to the sun, will create a range of seasonal roosting sites that the bats can use at will.

Never disturb bat boxes once they're in position – it's illegal and unkind. If you want to know whether your boxes are in use, watch quietly from a distance just before sunset and see if any fly out. You can also keep an eye open for droppings on the ground below the boxes – bat droppings are very like mouse droppings: dry and crumbly.

CLEANING NEST BOXES

It's a good idea to clean nest boxes once a year – though definitely not in spring. The end of summer/early autumn is probably the best time to aim for, when second broods have fledged. Lift the boxes down from their hanging positions and bring them out into the open. The old nests can be heavily infested with lice, mites, ticks and fleas, so tip old nesting material straight onto a bonfire or put it in the dustbin to reduce rates of reinfestation. Nests may also contain fungal spores that can irritate and infect human lungs, so always approach the job of cleaning with caution and aim to create the minimum amount of dust.

MAKING A BAT BOX

side

200mm (8 in)

140mm (5½ in.)

140mm (5½ in.)

200mm (8 in.)

side

side

330mm (13¼ in.)

back plate

140mm (5½ in.)

front

90mm (3½ in.)

base

200mm (8in.)

roof

Step 1 Start with a wooden board just over 1m (3ft) long and about 15cm (6in.) wide, and saw it into sections as marked. Use untreated timber.

Step 2 Make a groove in the back plate, about 5cm (2in.) from the top, to take the lid.

Step 3 Screw the sides, base, and back together. Add a narrow batten to the lower edge of the inside of the lid for a snug fit, before screwing the lid in place (unlike a bird box, you don't need a lid that opens).

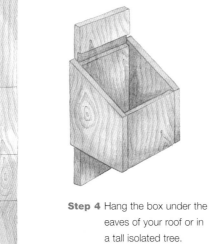

Step 4 Hang the box under the eaves of your roof or in a tall isolated tree.

What you need:
Piece of wood measuring approximately 1029mm x 152mm (40½in x 6in.).

tape measure

pencil

drill

rubber or metal hinge

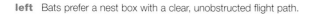

left Bats prefer a nest box with a clear, unobstructed flight path.

Making a pond

Probably the single most important change you can make to your garden to attract wildlife is to build a pond. Here you'll find information on the ideal depth for a pond, construction methods, pond linings, filling a pond with water, and pumps and fountains.

The decision about a site is one of the most important factors when you are making a garden pond. Ideally, the site should be in sun for most of the day but with a small section in shade, to keep an area of water cool in high summer. Shade can come from a nearby fence or wall, from a specially sited trellis plus climber, or from a tall pondside reed or rush.

above Water lilies not only look beautiful in bloom but provide shade and hiding places for pond creatures.

left A large stretch of water increases the range of habitats you can create.

Shade from a tree is less desirable. Trees and ponds are not a good combination for two reasons. First, digging a pond close to a tree will inevitably mean hitting tree roots, which can damage the tree, while any new root growth can puncture the pond lining. Second, autumn leaves drifting into the pond rot down and produce methane gas, which is toxic to pondlife. Even evergreen trees still lose leaves from time to time and falling pine needles can turn pond water acidic with lethal results for wildlife.

The site for your pond absolutely has to be a level piece of ground – trying to dig a pond on a slope and compensate for changes in level is tricky and if you get it wrong the resulting pond, with a seemingly sloping surface, will annoy you every time you look at it.

Don't forget that you want to enjoy the pond too – you may want make sure that you can see it from the patio or a window of the house. An area of decking close to the pond, with a bench, will allow you to appreciate it even more.

If you have space for a lake – and a big budget – you can plan a really grand affair with an island for nesting wildfowl, willow and alder beds round the edges, and a jetty for humans to enjoy the water too. To increase the habitat potential, a big space lends itself to a series of ponds of different depths, all interconnected but offering different aquatic habitats: deep water for big fish and for waterfowl; shallow water for invertebrates such as insect larvae and species like water scorpions, and even temporary ponds that dry up in summer.

DIGGING THE HOLE

Provided the ground isn't frozen, winter is quite a good time to construct a pond and, with any luck, you'll have it ready for the first frogs, toads and newts emerging from hibernation. (Planting up the pond, however, is best left until spring – few garden centres have pond plants for sale during winter months as the plants themselves will have died right back and you'd get the impression you were simply buying a pot of mud.)

There's no minimum ideal pond size but a pond of roughly 1.2m (4ft) by 75cm (2½ft) will give you the scope to include a section of 'deep' water for plants such as water lilies that like to sit in at least 60cm (2ft) of water, a shallower section for growing marginal plants that like their feet in water, and a gradually sloping 'beach' to allow wildlife easy access to and from the water. A deep spot will also allow pondlife to overwinter safely, even if the surface of the pond freezes. Remember that to end up with a pond 60cm (2ft) deep, you'll need to dig it considerably deeper, to allow for the thickness of the soft protective layer below the lining (see below). Another 12.5–15cm (5–6in) ought to do it.

In a wildlife garden, an irregular shape will always look the most natural – using a length of rope or hose to mark out the pond's shape will help achieve a natural look. To get a more three-dimensional impression of how the pond will look from different vantage points in the garden, add some vertical canes or sticks to mark out the outline. Leave these in place for a few days and keep staring at them – you'll probably end up shifting some until you're happy with the effect.

An irregular-shaped pond such as this will require a flexible liner (see page 79). However, it is also possible to buy preformed rigid liners in a variety of irregular shapes.

A circular, square or rectangular pond can be constructed using either a flexible liner, or a preformed rigid liner as shown on page 77.

If you're excavating a pond in a lawn, it's worth skimming off the turf first, as it may come in useful for edging the pond in places. Start by digging out small sections of the pond at a time, keeping the topsoil in a separate pile for reusing in raised beds or permanently sited containers (it makes temporary planters too heavy to move easily). Pile the subsoil – it's harder, stonier, drier – separately. You can add a layer of subsoil to the very base of the pond for bottom-rooting plants like water crowfoot, as it is low in nutrients and won't produce excessive algal growth; or use it to weigh down the edges of the liner where you want to create a bog garden. You can buy special low-nutrient pond compost for this job but, since you're excavating the subsoil anyway, you may as well make use of it.

Any pond much over 5m (16ft) in length will need a mechanical digger to get the job done, but whatever method you use, watch out for buried cables and piping.

Once you've got the basic shape dug out, check the level of a small pond by laying a board across the hole and using a spirit level. To prepare the base of the hole for the lining, rake over the soil and pick out sharp stones, bits of tree root and anything that might puncture the lining. To protect the lining further, you can add a layer of something soft at this stage. Sand is the traditional material but, if you have some old carpet or carpet underlay, surplus fibreglass roofing insulation or even a stack of newspapers for recycling, all these will do just as well. Bring this soft layer up over the edge of the pond, as the exposed edge is vulnerable to damage too.

CREATING A POND WITH A PREFORMED LINER

Step 1 Once you've dug your hole, you need to line it. Sand is the traditional material for creating a soft layer to protect the liner against puncture, but if you have old carpet, underlay or insulation, recycle that instead.

Step 2 If you're using a preformed liner like this formal rectangular pool, use a spirit level to check that it's level before you fill it with water – though you may need to run in a little for stability.

Step 3 You need to backfill around a preformed liner with sand, or sieved excavated soil.

Step 4 Lay the turf or edging stones while the pond is filling with water. This pond has a useful shallow-water 'shelf' around the edge for marginal plants.

Step 5 When edging a pond with slabs, it's vital that they are level—you don't want anyone to fall in the water.

Step 6 Set the slabs on coarse sand so that they overhang the margin of the pond and protect the soft liner below.

Step 7 Spread some cement where any of the liner is still visible, then cover with a sprinkling of gravel.

Step 8 Leaving larger gaps between some slabs creates planting pockets that allow you to grow plants right up to the water's edge.

CHOOSING A POND LINING

In a small garden, a preformed pond liner is ideal because manufacturers make allowances for the need for a shallow end plus planting ledges at various depths. The main disadvantage is getting the hole to be the right shape: it can be a bit tricky and generally involves some backfilling and adjusting.

Before the development of flexible lining sheets, concrete was a popular choice for making a pond, but it has a tendency to crack and is hard to work with—you have to get it right before it hardens. Making a pond using the ancient method of puddled clay may be an option if you have the right heavy soil, but importing the clay and the subsequent hard work—literally trampling it into a watertight layer—is a labor of love. Butyl- and rubber-based liners are much easier to use. Both are stretchy and supple, making it easy to fit them to irregular-shaped ponds. They come in a variety of grades and prices and are sold by the square foot.

To figure out how much you need to buy, measure the pond at its widest point and then measure the depth at its deepest. The total width you need to buy is the width of the pond plus twice the depth. Similarly, to get the length measurement, measure the pond at its longest point and add twice the depth. If you want to extend the liner into the surrounding soil to create a boggy area, add the appropriate amount to each measurement. Multiply the width and length measurements together to get the total area in square feet.

LAYING FLEXIBLE LINER AND ADDING WATER

Unfold the liner on the lawn and get someone to help you carry it across and lay it over the pond. Let the liner sag down into the hole and sift a layer of subsoil—no more than one to two inches (2.5–7.5cm) —to hold it in place. If the pond is so big that you have to stand in it to work, it's best to do so in bare feet to avoid damaging the lining. At the very least, check your boots for any sharp stones embedded in the soles.

Then it's time to fill the pond. Rainwater is the best option, but won't be practical for a large pond. Tap water tends to be heavily chlorinated but by leaving a pond filled with tap water alone for a few days, most of the chlorine will evaporate and it will be safe to plant. If you are using subsoil to cover the liner, you don't want the water gushing in and washing it all off, because it is not likely to settle back evenly. Instead, run the hose at a steady trickle, diffusing its flow by resting the end on an old cloth.

Once the pond is full, you can deal with the overlapping liner at the edges. For a boggy margin to the pond, bury the liner under five to six inches (12.5–15cm) of subsoil. Use subsoil again because water will run off it into the pond, and the nutrients in richer soil can cause problems with algae. To create solid edges you can walk on, use paving slabs or bricks, or re-lay any turf that you have skimmed off. A mixture of margins to a pond makes it usable for both wildlife and humans who want to watch what's going on.

PUMPS AND FOUNTAINS

A pump-operated fountain will keep water clear and well-oxygenated but if you have frog eggs in your pond, you will have to stop running the pump before the tadpoles hatch, otherwise they get sucked into the intake inlet and mashed up. You can run it again later in the season when the tadpoles are big enough and strong enough to resist being sucked in.

Planting up a pond

Make your pond as attractive to wildlife as possible by mimicking nature and adding a selection of marginal, floating and submerged plants.

Once you've filled the pond, leave it to settle for a week or so, to allow the silty subsoil to settle and chlorine in tap water to be driven off. Then it's time to start planting. Begin with the deep-water species such as water lilies. As with all wildlife-friendly planting, native species are best. Native water lilies such as *Nuphar lutea* are smaller flowered than nursery hybrids, but are very adaptable and will thrive in still or running water. They root in the bottom silt and send leaves and flowers up to the surface. Most water lilies are vigorous plants and can seriously crowd a pond – one giveaway signal is the plant sending up leaves well above the water surface when there is literally no more space for a lily pad to float. If you are starting with limited space, one method of confining water lilies is to grow them in perforated planting baskets that sit on the bottom of the pond.

Submerged oxygenating species such as curly pondweed, hornwort and water starwort, can either be left to float freely in the water or can be anchored to the bottom of the pond with small, smooth stones to encourage them to root. These plants are oxegenators supplying the wildlife in the plant with a vital supply of that gas.

By growing some tall plants in the shallow water at the pond's edge you can create a sheltered corridor that leads from the wider garden into the pond so that small creatures can safely travel between the two – newly emerged froglets are vulnerable to birds at this stage, for example, and giving them a bit of cover increases their chances of survival.

Step 1 Using a layer of small stones or rubble is one way of anchoring a liner in position in a turf-edged pond or one that features an adjoining bog garden.

Step 2 Match pond plants to different water levels. Water lilies are deep water plants; meadowsweet, mint, and flag irises prefer boggy borders or shallow water at the pond's edges.

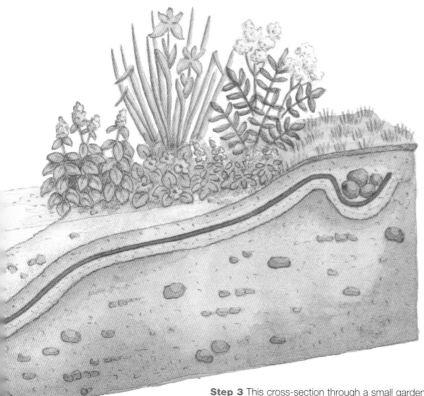

Step 3 This cross-section through a small garden pond shows how the depth varies as well as the position of the liner and the protective layer between it and the soil.

PLANTS FOR YOUR POND

Plants for water up to 15cm (6in) deep
*Brooklime (*Veronica beccabunga*)
*Flag iris (*Iris pseudacorus*)
Lesser spearwort (*Ranunculus flammula*)
Water mint (*Mentha aquatica*)

Tall plants for a boggy pond border
*Hemp agrimony (*Eupatorium cannabinum*)
*Meadowsweet (*Filipendula ulmaria*)
Purple loosestrife (*Lythrum salicaria*)
Ragged robin (*Lychnis flos-cuculi*)

Smaller plants for a boggy pond border
Bugle (*Ajuga reptans*)
Creeping Jenny (*Lysimachia nummularia*)
*Fleabane (*Pulicaria dysenterica*)
*Marsh marigold (*Caltha palustris*)

Oxygenating plants
Curly pondweed (*Potamogeton crispus*)
Hornwort (*Ceratophyllum demersum*)
Common starwort (*Callitriche stagnalis*)

Deep-water plants
Amphibious bistort (*Polygonum amphibium*)
*Water crowfoot (*Ranunculus aquatilis*)
*Yellow water lily (*Nuphar lutea*)

* indicates plant is featured in directory

Pond creatures

Lying full-length on the grass gazing into the depths of a pond is one of the best ways to appreciate its varied population.

If you add a bucket of oxygenating pondweed to a new pond, probably the first signs of life you'll notice will be water fleas shooting to and fro in a patch of sunlit water. Many flying insects lay their eggs in water, so a pond is likely to be home to a variety of insect larvae. Probably the most spectacular are dragonfly nymphs, which are quite ugly and fiercely predatory, making short work of a tadpole. When it is time for them to metamorphose into shiny, winged adults, they climb up a tall plant such as a flag iris stem until they are clear of the water.

Both adult diving beetles and their larvae are equally predatory, feeding on tadpoles and even small fish, so a small pond won't be able to support too many.

Gnats and mosquitoes have aquatic larval stages, so ponds are a favourite hunting ground for bats and swallows that feast on the newly emerged adults.

Unlike land snails, water snails are positively welcome in a pond, where they graze on unsightly algal blooms that fuzz up plant stems or coat the pond lining. They lay hundreds of eggs in jelly (a bit like frogspawn) on the underside of leaves, which hatch into tiny, perfect, baby snails.

Frogs, toads and newts all need water to breed in and the resulting tadpoles and small fry may in turn become prey to grass snakes, which are good swimmers.

What you don't need to do to any wildlife pond is add fish, especially goldfish. They will eat tadpoles and other desirable creatures and disturb the natural balance of the pond. Goldfish also tend to make the water murky as they stir up the silt at the bottom when feeding.

right Dragonflies spend their larval stage underwater.

DEALING WITH BLANKET WEED AND ALGAL BLOOMS

Until it settles down, a new pond is prone to becoming choked with blanket weed or similar slimy algae. Depending on the size of the pond, you can try raking out the blanket weed and leaving it on the side of the pond for a few hours so that any creatures scooped up can escape, before putting it on the compost heap. In small ponds it's quite satisfying to dip a stick in and keep twirling it so that the long filaments of blanket weed wrap round and round the twig like candy floss. Garden centres also sell mats of barley straw to float on the water. These are thought to help reduce algal growth by a chemical reaction that is harmless to other plants and pondlife.

above Densely planted ponds provide the richest, safest habitat for pond creatures.

Lily pads create shelter and camouflage for creatures such as frogs.

Maintaining a wildlife friendly garden

In many ways there is far less general garden maintenance to do in a wildlife garden. For a start there is a lot less tidying up to do. Dead flower stems create valuable hiding places for overwintering insects, and seedheads feed seed-eating birds.

You'll still need to water newly established plants and you may have to weed areas too, until new plants are strong enough to hold their own against opportunistic incomers. Here you'll find traditional gardening methods adapted where necessary to take into account the needs of garden wildlife.

Planting a tree

If you are investing in some expensive shrubs or trees or a row of hedging, you'll want to do a good job and give your investment a proper foundation from which to grow. Deciding to plant a tree is a major undertaking and you really only have one chance to get it right, so it makes sense to do it properly, especially as even a small tree can be an expensive investment.

FIRST, DIG YOUR HOLE

To make things easier, the planting hole needs to be bigger than the tree's root ball so that you can see what you're doing and have room to manoeuvre. Pile the soil in a heap to one side. If you dig so deeply that you hit subsoil – you'll know when you do because it's much harder to dig and looks thinner and poorer – try to keep the two soil types separate. (You don't want the subsoil to go back in the planting hole; it could be reused to make a meadow that needs poor soil, see page 122.)

Use a garden fork to rough up the base of the hole so that water drains easily and then tip in a layer of home-made compost or well-rotted manure.

TO STAKE OR NOT TO STAKE?

This is the point to add a stake if you are going to use one, but it's a tricky question to answer. Evergreen trees are more likely to need staking, for example, because their leaves present a large surface area to the wind, making the tree more vulnerable to being blown over. Any new tree on an exposed site will benefit from a bit of extra support until its root system gets established – but staking is only ever a temporary measure until the roots take over. To get them growing strongly, they need to feel, the effect of the wind. That is why a short stake is the best solution – it will support the lower portion of the tree but allow the top to move and thicken up and strengthen. Hammer in the stake to one side of the hole, then lower in the tree.

FILLING UP

Look to see where the soil mark comes on the tree: to get this level with the ground you may need to backfill the hole with some topsoil and then sit the tree roots on this. Spread out the tree's roots carefully. Fork some more manure or compost into the heap of topsoil and work it in around the roots, stopping to firm it with the ball of your foot to get rid of any air pockets.

Rather than making the soil surface around the trunk flat, finish it off so that the soil slopes inwards towards the tree trunk – this will direct water right to where it's needed instead of letting it run off.

Finally, use a proper tree tie to attach the tree to its stake (if using one). Rubber tree ties present damage to the bark and trunk caused by rubbing, but still need checking from time to time to make sure they are not cutting into the trunk or restricting its growth.

PLANTING WHIPS

If you have the space to create a small glade of trees, the easiest way to do it is by planting two-year-old saplings. Many native tree species are sold in this way and are far cheaper than pot-grown specimens.

To plant them in prepared dug-over soil, simply insert a spade and wiggle it back and forwards to make a wide slit. Lift the spade out and slide a whip in, then firm it in with the ball of your foot. Keeping the area weed-free until the small trees are well established gives them the best chance of success.

Step 1 Dig in some well-rotted, sieved, home-made compost to prepare the soil before planting.

Step 2 Make the planting hole at least as wide and deep as the container the tree is growing in.

Step 3 Plant the tree at the same depth as it was growing in the pot, adjusting the depth of the hole by adding or removing soil.

Step 4 Fill the planting hole with excavated soil, gently firming it down as you go.

Step 5 Staking a newly planted tree will help keep it in position until its root system is properly established.

Step 6 Once in position, the plant can be pruned.

Planting a hedge

Planting a hedge is one of the easiest ways to introduce a selection of wildlife-friendly shrubs into the garden. For maximum benefit to wildlife, make your hedge largely from native species. In a mixed hedge you can include a range of shrubs with different attributes – berries, blossom, and evergreen leaves for shelter. A single-species hedge can be just as good provided the plant has something to offer in each season.

FIRST, BUY YOUR PLANTS

The cheapest way to buy hedging plants is as bare-root whips. These are young saplings (usually two years old) that have been field grown then are lifted and sold in bundles during the dormant winter months. As well as being economical to buy they also establish well, having been used to tough conditions in the field. Look in the small ads in the back of gardening magazines or newspapers to find nurseries specialising in hedging plants.

For a dense hedge, you get best results by planting a double staggered row of saplings. To work out how many plants you need, aim to plant a sapling every 45cm (18in) – then double that quantity to get the final number.

A stable wild hedge mixture would be typically 50 per cent hawthorn with other species mixed in – such as holly, hazel, blackthorn, buckthorn, field maple, dogwood, guelder rose (*Viburnum opulus*), crab apple, spindle or damson – at a ratio of 10 per cent each.

STARTING FROM SCRATCH

Clear the ground of weeds or turf. Start by digging a trench about 60cm (2ft) wide and 45cm (18in) deep, piling the soil to one side. Then make a layer of well-rotted manure or home-made compost in the bottom of the trench to give the new plants a good start.

Lay out the first row of plants, each one 45cm (18in) away from its neighbour, setting them just in from the edge of the trench. Then add the plants for the second staggered row, planting them in between those for the first row and 30cm (12in) behind them. In a big garden where space is no object, you can make the two rows up to 1m (3ft) apart. This will create a sort of wildlife corridor that could be as much as 3m (10ft) wide when all the shrubs are mature, making a protected habitat within its boundaries for mammals and birds.

Backfill the trench with the excavated soil, holding each sapling upright as you fill around it. You should be able to see how deep each sapling was planted by looking at the stem for a sort of tide mark. Keep the soil at this depth. Go back over the soil, gently firming in each plant with the ball of your foot.

KEEP THE COMPETITION DOWN

Although the ultimate aim is to have a mature hedge with wildflowers at the base and climbers scrambling through, at the very beginning wild plants will compete closely with the young hedge shrubs for nutrients and water. Weed regularly or mulch to help get the hedge well established, and only then allow hedgerow plants to grow up.

Step 1 Before planting, line up the plants in their final positions approximately 45cm (18 in.) apart to gauge the effect. Keep to this distance when planting, using a ruler if necessary, and measuring from trunk to trunk.

Step 2 Lift plant from its pot, keeping its stake in position, and set in the planting hole. Push the soil back around it. Firm the soil gently round the base of the trunk with your hands.

Step 3 Scatter some bonemeal fertilizer round the newly planted shrubs. (Follow manufacturer's instructions for quantity to use.) Or use well-rotted manure or homemade compost. Fork the fertilizer or manure gently into the surface of the soil.

Step 4 Water well then mulch the plants with a moisture-retaining mulch such as chipped bark, or use a thick layer of well-rotted manure or homemade compost instead.

IDEAL HEDGING PLANTS

Beech (*Fagus sylvatica*)

Berberis (*Berberis* spp.)

Blackthorn (*Prunus spinosa*)

Buckthorn (*Rhamnus cathartica*)

Cotoneaster (*Cotoneaster* spp.)

Crab apple (*Malus sylvestris*)

Dog rose (*R. canina*)

Elder (*Sambucus nigra*)

Field maple

Hawthorn (*Crataegus* spp.)

Hazel (*Corylus avellana*)

Holly (*Ilex* spp.)

Hornbeam

Privet

Rosa glauca

Rosa rubiginosa

Rosa rugosa

Spindle (*Euonymus europaeus*)

Viburnum (*Viburnum*)

Yew (*Taxus baccata*)

Optional extras for colourful blossom

Forsythia

Flowering currant

Mock orange

Growing your own

Raising plants from seed is one of the most satisfying garden tasks.

SOWING STRAIGHT INTO THE GARDEN

This is the most straightforward way to grow plants from seed and is usually a spring job. The first step is to choose the right site: most annuals, for example, need full sun, while a sheltered spot will benefit visiting insects when the plants are in full bloom.

Prepare the soil by digging out any old roots and weeds. Then rake it to get rid of stones and lumps of earth. Planting in drifts creates the best habitat for bees and butterflies, and there are two ways to achieve this. Simply scatter the seed randomly within your prepared space – it's best not to do this in windy weather – and then rake the soil very lightly to barely cover the seed. Alternatively, sow seed conventionally in straight furrows within the prepared area. Simply pulling a short stick through the earth will create a deep enough furrow or drill and the seed can then be sprinkled thinly in the drill and the soil gently raked over. The straight line method is probably better for growing unfamiliar plants that you've never tried before – if seedlings are appearing in a straight line, you can be pretty sure they're your plants and not weeds that need removing.

Water the ground after sowing with a fine rose on a watering can – the aim is not to wash the seed away with a vigorous drenching. If you're worried about this happening, try watering the soil before sowing the seed.

Many annuals are fast-germinating – marigolds and candytuft, for example, will be through the soil in a matter of days in the right conditions. Perennial seeds can be slower.

STARTING PLANTS OFF INDOORS

For early-blooming flowers you can get a head start by sowing seed indoors – either on a spare windowsill in the house or in a greenhouse if you have one. It's a bit more fiddly than sowing direct in the garden, but a combination of the two can have a positive effect on insect wildlife (see page 117, Boosting Flower Production). Garden centres sell seed trays that come with a clear plastic lid to keep in moisture and warmth, and a drip tray to protect household surfaces. For best results use a potting compost sold specifically for seed; wet the compost before filling the tray and then sow the seed thinly.

When seedlings germinate the first pair of leaves to appear are the seed leaves, which are quite different from the plant's true leaves. When the latter have started to grow, is the signal to prick out seedlings into larger containers or individual mini pots, to give them more room.

ACCLIMATIZING INDOOR PLANTS OUTDOORS

Plants shifted from the protection of being grown indoors or in a greenhouse would simply die of shock if planted straight out into the garden or, even if they didn't die, their growth rate would be severely set back, negating the whole point of starting them off indoors in the first place.

This is where the hardening-off process comes in. Start by leaving pots or trays of plantlets outside for several hours on a sunny day, but bring them back in at night. Gradually leave them out for longer and longer periods before taking the big step and letting them stay out all night. Depending on the weather this could take one to two weeks.

left Sowing seed in small pots indoors gets plants off to an early start.

below left Once seedlings have formed several pairs of true leaves, they'll start to grow rapidly and will need potting on into larger individual pots.

below right If you're serious about growing from seed, it's a good idea to build up a range of different sized plantpots.

TIPS

• Water seedlings with water that has been kept at room temperature.

• Handle seedlings by their seed leaves when pricking out – not by their stems, which are far more easily damaged.

• Don't let small seedlings dry out – seed compost is notoriously difficult to re-wet when it dries out.

• Equally, don't overwater either – it's just as bad.

Watering

While a wildlife-friendly garden may require less maintenance than a formal one – less cutting back, tidying up and mowing – the one thing you still have to do is water it.

If you're interested in developing a wildlife-friendly plot, the chances are you are already very aware of conservation issues – and one commodity that we can all reuse and recycle is water. Rainwater butts are one way of collecting – even a butt connected to a shed roof will collect a reasonable amount. Keeping a lid on a butt prevents small animals and children suffering mishaps and will stop mosquitoes using the water as a breeding site. A lid also stops twigs and leaves falling into the butt and then clogging up the tap at the bottom.

You can even collect household waste water in a butt by inserting a diverter – a short length of pipe – into the bathroom waste-water pipe to divert water into the butt. If you're going to do this, keep bubblebaths to a minimum and use the water as quickly as possible. (If your bathroom is on the ground floor, simply try siphoning off the bathwater onto the garden.) Incidentally, it's generally not recommended to use household waste water on the vegetable plot or on any edible crop.

WHAT TO WATER

Plants are most vulnerable to stress from lack of water when they are small and newly planted, and their roots systems haven't fully developed. So new plantings are your top priority, especially young trees and hedges. Keep these well watered in the first few years and they will send down strong, healthy roots that will fend for themselves in subsequent years.

left Match plants to your garden – a hot, dry site calls for drought-resistant verbenas, mulleins and prairie grasses, which need little water once established.

There are various tricks for directing water straight to where it's needed. One is to make a shallow depression in the soil after planting a new tree or shrub (see page 86); another is to sink an inverted cut-off plastic drinks bottle into the soil when you plant and pour water into this rather than onto the surrounding soil, so that it sinks straight down to root level.

'Little and often' may be a good maxim to garden by, but it's not applicable to watering. It's better to give a plant a thorough soaking once a week with a whole watering can full of water than to give it a light sprinkle every day. The latter keeps the roots close to the surface instead of encouraging them to grow downwards in search of moisture.

Plants growing in pots need water most of all, and may need watering morning and evening in very hot weather. If you let the compost in a container dry right out, it can be very difficult to re-wet it, especially if the compost has shrunk away from the sides of the pot – then all that happens when you water is that the water runs down the gap and straight out of the bottom. If this happens, you will need to stand the pot in a bucket of water for an hour or so until the compost rehydrates.

WHEN TO WATER

The traditional time to water the garden is in the cool of the evening, especially after a long, hot day when plants are likely to have become stressed through lack of water. Early morning is a good time too, to boost plants for the coming day. There is also some scientific evidence that watering vulnerable small plants early in the day makes them less prone to slug or snail attack, perhaps because the molluscs are already hiding for the day. Watering in the evening, when they are active, may simply attract them to plants by creating the conditions that slugs and snails like.

Whichever end of the day you find most convenient, the one thing you must never do is water on a hot day in full sunshine. However careful you are, you are bound to splash the leaves, and in intense sun these droplets can act like a magnifying glass, and actually scorch a plant's leaves. Also, on a day that is so hot that plants have wilted, no amount of water will make them recover until the temperature cools, so any watering done before this is a waste of effort.

WATER TEMPERATURE

Collecting water in barrels and tubs has another big advantage besides its environmental merits – it is already at ambient temperature. Using cold water straight from the tap to water plants on a hot day can literally shock them. If you have to use mains water, be prepared – fill your cans early in the day and let them stand in a sunny spot to warm up.

LACK OF WATER

Lack of water affects plants in all sorts of ways, some more obvious than others. Easiest to spot is straightforward wilting, when leaves droop and stems keel over from the lack of rigidity that water confers. But the ramifications for wildlife are more subtle. A plant in full bloom needs water to make sure every flower is full of nectar, and a plant under stress from a lack of water produces much less nectar, affecting visiting bees and butterflies. Once the flowers are spent, lack of water can seriously affect the development of fruit and berries and, if a

berry crop is reduced, birds will have to search elsewhere for a food source.

above Using a butt or barrel to collect rainwater is simple, environmentally sound and good for plants too.

above right   If filling a watering can with tap water, leave it to warm up before using.

below right   The amount of nectar a flower produces drops when water is scarce.

left   Directing a spray of water at tough trees and shrubs, like this plum tree, can also help dislodge pests like aphids while watering the plant.

Feeding the soil and plants

In the wild there is a constant cycle of growth and decay so that dying plant material is broken down and returned to the soil as nutrients, along with dead bodies of wild creatures. Insects, fungi and smaller organisms such as bacteria assimilate decaying matter back into the soil.

In the garden this natural cycle tends to get interrupted as we sweep leaves off the lawn or clear away dead annuals from the borders. That's why it's still in order to 'interfere' in the wildlife-friendly garden by introducing external materials to improve the soil, such as manure and compost, and so boost the plants growing there.

MANURE

One of the best ways of adding nutrients to the soil and improving its condition at the same time is to dig in well-rotted manure. The key lies in the phrase 'well-rotted': all manure, whether from stables or farmyard, cannot be used fresh. Fresh manure uses up nitrogen as it rots, robbing the soil – and so the plants – of this vital nutrient in the process. Manure can be considered well rotted after it has been left to stand for about six weeks, preferably in a heap, firmed down to remove air pockets, and covered with plastic sheeting.

Manure from an organic source is the best but may be unavailable as it is too precious a resource for an organic farm to sell. Where you think manure may be tainted with chemicals, such as growth hormones, or where the straw in horse manure may have been treated with herbicides or pesticides, the best option is to leave the manure to stand for a year to give residues a chance to decompose.

IN A SMALL GARDEN

Where there's no space for a bulky manure heap, buy in ready-rotted manure in bags and use it straight away. If there isn't a stable nearby selling well-rotted manure, go to the local garden centre and see what's on sale. There is now a market in prepackaged manures such as organic pelleted chicken manure, which is much easier to use – and far less smelly – than the stuff straight from the hen house. Waste hops from brewing industries are also sold prepackaged, as is spent mushroom compost from mushroom farms. You can also buy concentrated liquid manures that are easy to store and can be mixed up in a watering can and applied to pots and flowerbeds.

HOW TO APPLY

On bare ground that you are turning into a flowerbed, dig in the manure to improve the soil. Well-rotted manure is a universal cure-all: it opens up and aerates heavy clay soils; on light, sandy soils it helps bind particles together and improves water retention. By applying manure as you dig the bed over before planting, you're putting the nutrients right where they are needed. On an existing bed with established perennials and shrubs, it's easier to apply the manure as a mulch (see page 100) and wait for soil organisms to do all the work for you as they turn over the soil and incorporate the manure.

top right In a large garden there's room for a sprawling manure heap whose contents can be used to enrich the soil as and when needed.

right Well-rotted manure can be added to planting holes when putting new plants in a border or spread as a mulch (see page 100).

PLANT-BASED LIQUID FEED

Comfrey is a wildflower that can be tucked into a corner under a hedge or by the dustbin or compost bin to stop it spreading too far. It is a useful bee plant, but when it has finished flowering in late spring it can be cut right down to ground level, and the foliage and stalks used to make a liquid feed that will boost flower and fruit production.

1. Hose down the cut stems with water and pack them into a bucket or even a water butt (if you've harvested a big stand of comfrey).

2. Put the lid on the butt or cover the bucket and leave the mixture for a month or so. The resulting liquid smells unbelievably awful but has potent properties.

3. Dilute it with water in the ratio of 1:6 and use it in the vegetable plot to feed tomatoes or beans; in a flower border it will give a boost to sweet peas, roses and other repeat-flowering plants.

You can also try this method with nettles if you have too many – you may need to actually add water rather than relying on just wetting the leaves and stems.

Compost

In all but the tiniest plots it should be possible to squeeze in a compost bin – the exceptions are balconies and terrace gardens, where it would be impractical to try.

Making compost has all sorts of benefits. You produce your own rich soil conditioner for free from household scraps. There's less waste for the bin men to collect each week, and depending on your garden size and type of compost heap or bin, the heap itself can become a wildlife habitat.

In a small garden, a compost bin is probably the best option – there are some very attractive wooden ones that look like old-fashioned beehives, but plastic ones do the job equally well and can be screened by a piece of trellis and a climber. In a large garden where there's space for an untidy heap, you may get grass snakes breeding in the warmth of the rotting material and small mammals like hedgehogs hibernating there in winter. Even if you don't get any of the bigger inhabitants, a compost heap is still alive with creepy-crawlies helping to break down the contents, while in turn becoming food for creatures higher up the food chain themselves. Soil organisms break down compost materials into rich humus just as they would on the woodland floor. Beetles, worms and woodlice burrowing through the heap make useful aeration channels and bacteria work to break down the materials, generating heat in the process.

MAKING A COMPOST HEAP

To get things going, all that's needed is to start a compost heap in contact with the soil. (In a compost bin, just add a little soil to the compost materials to start the process.)

Making a heap straight on the ground is easy when you have the space. First, dig a couple of shallow channels at right angles to each other,

making a cross shape, to help aerate the centre of the heap as it grows. Or simply lay some branches and twigs to form the base of the heap and allow air to penetrate. If you want to keep the heap contained in some way, build sides from scrap wood such as old pallets or fence panels.

above Flower borders produce compostable waste in the form of spent flowers and leaves, not to mention weeds.

right A neatly stacked compost heap with colourful new material added on top.

COMPOST INGREDIENTS

The basic rule of making good compost is to keep a balance between dry and wet ingredients.

What you can include

- All household scraps such as vegetable and fruit peelings, eggshells, teabags, coffee grounds
- Shredded paper and cardboard
- Natural materials such as old woolly socks, cotton T-shirts, cut into strips
- Annual weeds (see page 39)
- Pretreated perennial weeds (see page 39)
- Waste foliage from the vegetable plot
- Grass cuttings in moderation – mix them well with other ingredients, such as crumpled-up newspaper or cardboard; if grass cuttings overwhelm the compost heap they will make it slimy and smelly

What not to include

- Cooked food – attracts undesirables such as rats
- Meat or fish – attracts undesirables
- Twigs – they won't rot down and they'll end up annoying you, especially if you have to sieve the compost before you use it
- Autumn leaves – these rot down by a separate process that relies on fungi rather than bacteria and are best kept in their own pile

Mulching

Mulching – basically covering bare soil – has a number of benefits, and all of them are labour-saving, which is good news whatever your style of gardening.

Mulching can be a way of reducing the number of weeds that grow and so avoid the chore of weeding later on. It is also a technique for retaining moisture in damp soil so that you don't have to water so often. It can also be a method for clearing weed-infested land by smothering pernicious plants. Applied before winter it acts like a blanket, keeping the ground slightly warmer. And if you use an organic material as a mulch – rather than an inert material such as newspaper, plastic, landscape fabric, old carpet, etc. – then mulching is also a way of improving the soil.

MULCHING FOR LAND CLEARANCE

In a large garden where you have the luxury of time and space, mulching can be an effective way of ridding land of difficult weeds. Digging over a bed to rid it of weeds such as dock is often a waste of time since its long tap root is capable of regenerating from small pieces – the same is true of bindweed and other perennial plant pests. But if you can leave the ground for a year, smothered in tough black plastic (weighted down with bricks and stones to stop it wrapping itself around a neighbour's tree in the next high wind), nature will do the job for you. Old carpet will do the trick or even a very deep mulch of straw – at least 15cm (6in) – it all depends on what you have to hand.

MULCHING FOR WATER RETENTION

It should go without saying that it is pointless to mulch dry soil, so don't try this technique until after a good downpour. Choose your mulch to match the site: on a bed in a hot, sunny place planted with plants that tolerate dry conditions, gravel is a good choice; in a semi-shady border use bark chippings or home-made compost. Permeable mulches like these let more rainfall through – plastic is not an option for this method.

MULCHING FOR WEED PREVENTION

A nice thick mulch – at least 5cm (2in) deep – will stop the majority of weed seeds germinating by blocking out the light. You can use home-made compost, well-rotted farmyard manure, bark chippings, even grass cuttings (though spread these more thinly). The main proviso is to keep the mulch clear of existing plants and shrubs – leave a collar of space around them – mulching effectively raises the soil level, which can cause plant stems to rot where they come into contact with the mulch.

above If you can get it, seaweed makes a good mulch – it is rich in nutrients; all it needs is a quick rinse before you use it.

right A mulch of chipped bark conserves water and looks neat.

Pest control

In the early stages of establishing your wildlife garden, there are bound to be times when wildlife populations are still stabilizing and things get out of balance. You will notice a build-up of pests, because there aren't sufficient predators to deal with them.

Even when your garden is mature and established, you'll probably have to resort to some of the following techniques, some of the time. A garden is still an artificial habitat, no matter how close to nature you've tried to make it, and you'll still have to play God and interfere every now and then.

GREENFLY

Greenfly or aphids are instantly recognizable by their dense colonies that tend to target new shoots and buds. Their natural predators are ladybirds and their larvae (an adult ladybird can eat up to 5,000 aphids in its lifetime) hoverflies and their larvae, lacewings and their larvae, and small insect-eating birds such as bluetits. However, until these start doing their job, you may have to pitch in too.

It all depends on how big your garden is. In a small to average garden, you may be able to keep on top of the situation. Every time you pass a rose bush, for example, examine the growing tips and flower buds. If they are smothered with aphids, check first to see whether any predators are present too. Adult ladybirds, lacewings and hoverflies are easy enough to spot, but their larvae can be more tricky. Ladybird larvae are dark grey with pale spots and their bodies are divided into segments. Hoverfly larvae are simply maggot-like, while lacewing larvae can appear furry because of the clusters of feathery gills on each body segment – their bodies are broadly striped from top to tail. A single lacewing larva can eat up to 300 aphids before pupating into an adult. It will also tackle whitefly and red spider mite. Lacewing eggs are also very distinctive as they are laid on thin stalks.

If there's no sign of any of the above predators, it's time to do something. If you're not squeamish, take action and firmly sweep off the aphids from a rosebud, for example, with your fingers. Or, depending on the scale of the problem, use a jet of water to wash them off, or a paintbrush dipped in water. If you've seen bluetits in the garden, try enticing them down to deal with the problem by hanging titbits to tempt them, such as fat balls (see page 55), directly in the rose bushes.

It is possible to buy adult ladybirds by mail order if you think your garden is deficient, but solutions like this are more for environments such as greenhouses, where the insects are physically restricted – if you simply release them into your garden, what's to stop them flying next door? However, some wildlife garden product suppliers are now starting to offer ladybird and lacewing larvae, which can be released right on the site of the problem and are likely to stay put if conditions are right.

Ladybirds and their larvae, and hoverfly larvae, also prey on other insect pests, including scale insects and spider mites.

SLUGS AND SNAILS

Try looking at slugs and snails from a whole different viewpoint – as a vital food source for ground-feeding birds like thrushes, for amphibians like frogs, toads and slow worms, and for beautiful violet ground beetles and small mammals like hedgehogs and shrews. If things get seriously out of kilter at the beginning – if your hostas are being reduced to a latticework of ribs, for example – there are things you can still safely do. Not all of them work in every garden, but are worth a try.

One solution is to go out at night and pick off slugs and snails from hostas and lilies by torchlight, and then tip them all into the compost heap in the hope they'll stay there and help break down less precious plant materials. Put a small number in the garden pond – tadpoles readily attack slugs and snail corpses. If you have neighbours who keep chickens or ducks, offer them the slugs as a treat for their domestic fowl.

Another idea is to lay small pieces of wood, stone or even grapefruit halves, cabbage leaves or old potatoes on the soil for slugs and snails to retreat under during the day. Then go round each morning and overturn the 'shelters' and hope that thrushes will come along and feast on the exposed creatures.

PHYSICAL BARRIERS

Once they've reached a reasonable size, most plants won't be harmed by the odd nibbled leaf: they are at their most vulnerable when they are seedlings. To help them reach maturity, try using protective measures to minimize slug and snail damage. A mini cloche made from a cut-down plastic bottle can see small plants through the worst. Other gardeners swear by barriers that stop slugs and snails crossing the soil: encircle plants with crushed eggshells, soot or sharp sand. Plants in tubs and pots can be protected by barriers of copper tape, which is claimed to deter slugs and snails.

PESTS AND VEGETABLES

It's in the vegetable plot that gardeners are likely to experience the most conflicting emotions, when plants are being grown for food rather than pleasure and there's less of a sharing attitude.

There are several approaches to take. One is to use trial and error to find out which vegetable varieties appear to be less palatable to your local slugs and snails, and which seem less prone to insect attack. For example, red lettuces like lollo rosso may escape slug damage in your area. Ask friends and neighbours for their experiences.

Another is to experiment with companion planting: mixing flowers into the vegetable patch to attract beneficial insects right where they're needed. Introducing marigolds (both common marigolds, *Calendula officinalis*, and the French or African species, *Tagetes patula*) among the cabbages and beans will entice visiting hoverflies and wasps, which, then move on to deal with aphids and grubs.

Even simply breaking up monocultures by planting mixed rows of potatoes and broad beans can be enough to reduce pest attack. Whether this works by as yet undocumented chemical secretions or simply by confusing pests that prefer to attack plantings en masse doesn't really matter as long as it actually does help.

top left Slugs and snails are notoriously fond of hosta leaves, often reducing them to a skeleton of tough leaf ribs.

top right Adult ladybirds and their larvae will devour thousands of greenfly.

bottom left Aphids tend to congregate in inaccessible spots among buds, but ladybird, and other predatory larvae will follow them right in there.

bottom right Grapefruit halves (after you've eaten the contents) work like slug hotels, attracting them to spend the day resting beneath. Turn them over and let the birds do the rest.

The garden in winter

Essentially, in winter you should be doing very little in the garden, and certainly not any major landscaping work that will disturb overwintering wildlife.

As plants and animals shut down for the season, they don't want to be disturbed by an overzealous gardener. This is not the time to start tackling an untidy corner or shifting a pile of bricks or logs – any major tasks like this will disturb many hibernating creatures, from frogs to hedgehogs to all manner of insects. Resist the urge to tidy up: cutting down plant stems reduces shelter available for insects; taking out shrubs or even removing twiggy branches reduces cover and shelter for roosting birds.

Instead you can still do jobs such as sweeping paths and terraces, and keeping lawns free of debris – often simple tasks like these are enough to add definition to the garden and keep it looking cared for.

GETTING READY FOR WINTER

As the days grow shorter and colder, many creatures start looking for a sheltered place to spend the winter. As well as the habitats you have created in your garden, there are a number of extra steps you can take to help wildlife overwinter.

Laying twiggy prunings at the base of a hedge increases the habitat available to small creatures looking for shelter – leaves and debris soon build up against the twigs, creating ideal hibernating spots for spiders and insects.

Hollow stems

Leaving hollow plant stems in place in the border will mean that ladybirds, for example, have a place to spend the winter. If, for whatever reason, you have to cut stems down or they get blown over, just

above top Holly berries are an essential birdfood in winter.

above The safest way to melt water in a bird bath, without damaging the actual structure, is to stand a saucepan of hot water on the ice.

right A winter garden with all the right elements still in place – spent flower stems and plant skeletons gain elegance from a light frost, as well as sheltering wildlife and protecting next year's plants.

tuck them under a hedge or bush instead. A variety of plant stems become hollow as they age and die, including hollyhocks, sedum, sunflowers and many others. As well as leaving some in place, prepare others in advance to make your own insect hibernating chambers. Cut the stems into shorter, more manageable lengths if necessary, and bundle them together and tie with string. Tuck bundles into sheltered spots at the foot of a wall, fence or hedge to attract insects, including solitary bees. These will often nest in bundles of hollow stems over the summer, then seal up some chambers with mud to overwinter.

Help for bees

You can also buy bee-nest kits that consist of a plastic cylinder packed with narrow cardboard tubes. Manufacturers often recommend that you lift the nest, pack it in a cardboard box, and put it in an unheated shed until the following spring, which may be worth doing in areas prone to severe winters.

READY-MADE HIBERNATION BOXES

In a small garden with fewer suitable sites for overwintering insects, insect boxes can improve winter survival rates substantially.

Lacewings and ladybirds

Beneficial insects such as lacewings and ladybirds, which both prey on aphids, spend the winter tucked away in crevices and hollow plant stems. Often they

above left Spent flowerheads of ice plants (*Sedum spectabile*) still have a certain charm, while sheltering spiders and small insects.

below left Silky clematis seedheads contribute visually to the garden in winter, as well as providing mini habitats.

far left Once the sun has melted the frost, a lawn is still a prime hunting ground for birds, even in winter.

find their way indoors and are woken from hibernation by central heating or by a mild day. To encourage them to overwinter somewhere more suitable, you can buy ready-made insect houses. Designs suitable for both species generally have a sloping roof so that the rain runs off and a louvred front that allows the insects to crawl in. Some wildlife product specialists also sell chemical attractants based on insect pheromones, which you can add to make sure that the right inhabitants reach the insect house.

Butterflies

You can also buy butterfly boxes – wooden boxes with slits in the base for butterfly access – to supplement your garden habitat. Site them on creeper-covered walls for extra protection.

PONDLIFE

Before the weather gets too bad, thin out floating pond plants by raking out surplus plants and leaving them on the edge of the pond for a few hours. This way, any creatures inadvertently caught up with the pond plants can wriggle back into the water again (the surplus plant material can then go on the compost heap).

Ponds are inactive in winter, when most inhabitants sink to the bottom layer of silt to sit out the season. (The frogs, toads and newts that came to the pond to breed will have found a spot on land to hibernate, in a logpile or a heap of rocks.) Even so, it is not a good idea to let a thick layer of ice build up on a pond: it is still a living, breathing ecosystem and toxic waste gases can build up under the ice. One way to keep an air hole open is to float a ball on the water. The ice can't get a grip against the rounded sides, so there is always a gap around the ball.

To open an airhole in a frozen pond, bring an old saucepan full of water to the boil on the stove then fetch it out and sit it on the ice until the ice melts. You'll need to open an airhole daily during prolonged frozen spells.

Never attempt to smash a hole in the ice – the reverberating shockwaves through the ice and water can kill pondlife. Similarly, never use salt or antifreeze to melt the ice as they will kill pondlife and permanently affect the pond water.

above One of the benefits of leaving plant stems in place instead of cutting them down is the unexpected beauty they gain in a frost.

right A globe artichoke left to flower gains subtle tones in decay and makes an ideal overwintering spot for insects.

Pruning

Although pruning is often seen as a way of keeping plants in check, it also stimulates them into growth and can be used to make a bird-friendly habitat.

For every cut you make on a shrub, two or three shoots will sprout from that point. By taking advantage of this fact you can get dense, twiggy cover ideal for birds to nest in. With a newly planted hedge, you can create good cover low down by pruning the new young saplings to make them branch and bush out at the base.

Timing is critical when pruning hedges. Never do it during the nesting season, which means all work must be done by the start of spring. In fact, if you can afford the space, a mixed hedge of native species need only be pruned every couple of years. In a long run of hedging just run a chainsaw along the sides and top, and use a rake to remove the clippings from the top of the hedge. In areas of the country where there are heavy winters, shaping the hedge so that it is wider at the base than the top can avoid damage caused by heavy snowfall forcing branches down and opening up permanent gaps in the hedge. If the base is wider than the top, it gives upper branches more support from below.

CLEMATIS

Huge, sprawling clematis, varieties such as *Clematis montana*, are best left to their own devices where space allows, as their tangled, rampant growth produces the ideal habitat for nesting or roosting birds, and protective shelter for a vast range of insects and small mammals. If they have truly got out of hand, then cutting right back in autumn or winter will ensure regrowth in time for spring nesting.

ROSES

Climbing roses can become bare at the base, so to increase leaf cover lower down, cut back an old stem or two at ground level. This should stimulate the rose to send up new shoots from the base, increasing cover and shelter.

CREATING NEST SITES

The easiest time to do this is winter, when deciduous trees have lost their leaves and when there is no chance of disturbing nesting birds. What you are looking for is comfortable forks and 'vees' where birds can build a nest in relative safety. Where a tree's main stem branches, for example, you may be able to take out a branch to create a bowl-shaped join that is perfect for a nest. A judicious snip or two can improve the flight path to a hollow, or a hole or fissure in the stem.

Trees are important roosting places for birds too. Unbelievable though it may seem, in winter even a leafless tree can provide considerable advantages over roosting in the open. Bare branches and twigs can measurably reduce wind speed and help create a marginally warmer microclimate for roosting birds at night. Pruning to increase branching and twigginess can have a positive beneficial effect.

right *Clematis viticella* cultivars are tough, hardy climbers that can reach 6m (20ft) in height. Pruning them severely in late winter, before birds start nesting, will promote dense, vigorous spring growth.

COPPICING

Coppicing is an ancient woodland technique that developed as a way of harvesting timber for all sorts of purposes – fuel, fencing, building etc. It is based on the fact that most trees and shrubs will regrow if cut down. By cutting back a tree or shrub to ground level, you can use the wood and be sure of another crop in 10–15 years time. If you have an area of woodland to look after, coppicing is a valuable way of letting light into the canopy and of creating woodland at different stages by managing trees at different stages of growth – from mature uncut trees to recently cut; newly sprouting to those somewhere in between. These in turn create different habitats that will attract a wider range of birds and small mammals. Birds such as warblers, which like to nest in scrubby undergrowth, will be attracted to newly cleared patches where brambles can grow; other species such as nightingales prefer taller growth that is several years old.

For most gardeners, coppicing can be used in a small garden as a one-off technique to deal with a tree or shrub that has outgrown its position. By cutting a hazel or silver birch to within a few inches of the ground, you will temporarily let more light into the area and boost plant life. Within a few years you will have a multi-stemmed grove that makes an ideal bird habitat for nesting, roosting and feeding.

Although it seems drastic, coppicing kick-starts trees into growth – they can put on 30cm (1ft) in a year – and growth is healthier and stronger too.

SHRUBS

From a nesting bird's point of view, the bushier a shrub the better, and one way to achieve this is to lop off the top of a young shrub in winter, just below where it starts to fork. The resulting mass of new shoots must be pruned a little higher the following year to produce yet more forking branches that create a secure nesting site or 'cradle' in their midst.

right Use the right tool for the job – secateurs are fine for pruning thin stems like those on this plum tree.

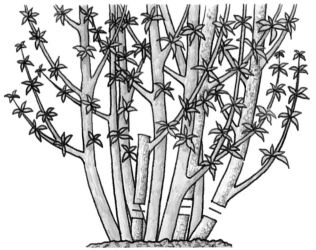

above To rejuvenate an old, overgrown shrub, take out about a third of the old stems, cutting them right back to ground level. Do this over three years – it's less of a shock than hacking back the whole bush in one go.

above Prune spring-flowering shrubs immediately after flowering to give the bush the maximum available time to produce flowering stems for next year. Cut back stems that have flowered, taking them back to the old wood. Both these techniques described will also boost flower production: see page 117.

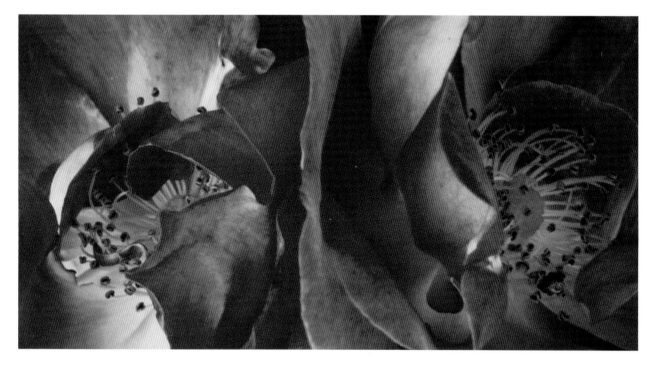

above Most roses need pruning to promote strong, healthy growth and to increase flowering.

Boosting flower production

There are a few gardener's tricks that you can use to get the maximum flowering potential from your garden, which will benefit visiting insects and improve your enjoyment too.

PRUNING

Pruning may seem like interfering too far with nature. After all, how do bushes get pruned in the wild? The answer is that they do, in a haphazard sort of way – by the wind, by animal damage, or by storm damage. In a managed habitat like a garden, pruning is necessary – and beneficial in many ways, not least an improvement of which is flowering.

There are no hard-and-fast rules, just some common-sense guidelines. First, you need to take into account when a shrub flowers.

SPRING FLOWERING

Prune a spring-flowering shrub in late winter and you won't see any flowers that year – they'll all have been removed in the process. Spring-flowering shrubs need pruning the minute they've finished flowering. Cut back the stems that have flowered – you should be able to spot new foliage starting to sprout lower down, and this is the point to cut back to. Older bushes can be stimulated into fresh new growth by taking out two or three stems completely, right back to ground level.

Some spring shrubs need very little pruning, for example ceanothus, lilac, daphne, skimmia and sarcococca, so go easy on these species.

left The aim of most flowering plants is to set seed. By constantly removing flower heads as they fade, you are thwarting this natural process and forcing the plant to produce more flowers.

MIDSUMMER FLOWERING

Late winter to early spring is the time to prune shrubs that flower from midsummer onwards, on new shoots that are produced in spring. Lavenders and hebes can be clipped over gently with shears without cutting back hard into old woody stems. Buddlejas, by contrast, can be brutally chopped down to ground level so that they send up fresh pliable stems bursting with flowers. Late-flowering roses need whole stems removed at the base to encourage new vigorous growth. New growth means improved flowering – that's more blossom to feed foraging bees and butterflies.

If you want to see the results of not pruning shrubs, this is easy to spot in a neglected garden: great woody buddlejas with bare stems and flowers only on the tips of the branches; lavender bushes that have gone spare and leggy with masses of old wood and dead leaves visible; bare, spiny rose stems with roses clustered sky-high out of enjoyment's reach.

GETTING MORE FLOWERS FROM ROSES

Climbing roses flower on side shoots from the main upright stems. The way to encourage the rose to produce more side shoots – and so more flowers – is to take the upright stems and train them to grow horizontally. The resulting upright side shoots can be pruned to stimulate them into producing flowering shoots themselves.

To train the stems horizontally it's easier if you grow the rose against a trellis-covered wall or a wall with a system of horizontal wires running across.

DEADHEADING

The aim of any plant, whether perennial, annual or shrub, is to ensure the survival of the next generation by setting seed. By cutting off the flower head and preventing the seed maturing – deadheading – the plant is conned into producing yet more flowers in a frantic attempt to set seed.

Deadheading works well with annuals such as sweet peas, antirrhinums, marigolds and cosmos. Just nip off flowers that are past their best with your fingernails or a pair of garden scissors. Smaller flowered plants like candytuft can be clipped over with shears.

It's only worth deadheading roses that are repeat-flowering, that is, that flower continuously over the summer. You'll need secateurs to do it properly and you should tail off deadheading activity towards the end of summer to get a reasonable crop of rosehips.

SECOND FLUSHES

Rather than deadheading for a continuous display of flowers, some species, especially perennials, can actually be cut right down to the ground – in some cases leaves and all – to promote a second flush of flowers later in the year.

This is a technique that works well with many species of hardy geranium, with delphiniums (flower stalk only) and thistles such as *Cirsium rivulare*.

SUCCESSIONAL SOWING

Even the most assiduous deadheading won't keep a plant in flower for ever but there is another trick for extending the flowering season of annuals. Successional sowing involves sowing seed of the same species at regular intervals – typically every two to three weeks up until early summer.

The easiest way to sow hardy annuals is straight into the ground. Sow annuals in drifts to make life easier for visiting bees and butterflies, and just keep adding a couple of lines of seed every few weeks. You'll end up with fresh new plants coming into flower in stages over the summer. To really get a head start with early flowering, many hardy annuals can be sown in autumn: they'll still have time to make tough little plants to overwinter and get going fast again in spring. Marigolds, sweet peas, cornflowers, love-in-a-mist, scabious, candytuft and poached egg plant can all be started off in autumn.

above Roses can be kept in bloom for longer by deadheading – cutting off spent flowers before they have time to set seed.

right Lavender will flower better if pruned lightly in spring.

Lawns and grass

People and wildlife – especially birds – like grass. And it is possible to have a family-friendly lawn that attracts wildlife too.

GARDEN LAWNS

Compared to a species-rich meadow, a traditional garden lawn may seem a surprising asset in a wildlife garden, but what it offers is an open viewing space for birds. A closely cut lawn is still a good feeding place for birds – sit and watch and you'll see blackbirds and thrushes search for worms; after a rainy night starlings will be out in force diligently searching for grubs. Later in the year some birds will be after grass and weed seeds, and you can improve their chances of finding them simply by raising the mower blades and mowing a little less frequently. This will also allow flowers to bloom in the grass.

This technique is the best compromise for a family garden where a flat lawn to play on is still an important element.

Leave the lawn alone and after a few weeks low-growing daisies will start to flower and sky-blue speedwell flowers will be visible in the grass. There may be tiny two-lipped purple selfheal (*Prunella vulgaris*) flowers and soft, fluffy yellow cat's ears (*Hypochaeris radicata*). The irony is that, to keep them flowering, you do have to start mowing again, otherwise the grass grows too tall and overshadows them. This type of flowery lawn is probably the best option for a tiny garden, introducing variety into the grass that will benefit bees and birds but still make a usable lawn for the family.

above This lawn has been left to grow slightly wild and will attract many birds and butterflies.

right In this garden a lawn has been used in place of a traditional pathway and tulips have been planted.

MAKING A MEADOW

An ancient meadow rich in wildflowers may have taken centuries to reach a flowering balance. To expect to achieve similar results in a garden within a few seasons is clearly unrealistic but it's definitely worth experimenting to see what you can do.

Where you have a bit more space, you can try leaving an area of lawn unmown and see which wildflowers move in or were already there in seed form but unable to germinate. Typically these might include yarrow (*Achillea millefolium*), lady's smock (*Cardamine pratensis*), tall ox-eye daisies (*Leucanthemum vulgaris*) and meadow buttercups (*Ranunculus acris*).

SPRING MEADOWS

The time of year when you mow a meadow area will control the wildflowers that grow there – if you cut a species down before it has set and scattered seed, there is less chance that it will grow again the next year. The main choices are between a spring meadow and a summer one.

In a spring meadow, mowing has to be delayed until spring wildflowers have bloomed and set seed – usually by the start of summer. Then after the first cut, the meadow can be mowed regularly until late autumn. This regime will give you a usable lawn all summer long – invaluable in a family garden – and a sward of flowers in spring.

A spring meadow is ideal if you want to naturalize spring bulbs such as crocuses, grape hyacinths, small daffodils and fritillaries. Delaying mowing until early summer gives the bulbs a chance to build up reserves for next year's flowers before their leaves are mown off.

SUMMER MEADOW

In a summer meadow the mowing pattern is to cut regularly until early summer and then leave everything to grow up and flower, starting cutting again at the beginning of autumn, rather like a traditional hay meadow on a farm. To maintain the meadow soil's low fertility you must rake off the 'hay' from the first cut and use a box to pick up all subsequent clippings. Pet rabbits and guinea pigs will appreciate home-grown hay.

STARTING FROM SCRATCH

Unlike almost all other areas of the garden, the best results for a meadow-type lawn will be on poor, unimproved soil. If you've recently excavated a pond, a meadow planting is the perfect use for all the subsoil that was dug out. Depending on quantity, it could be landscaped into a low mound or used to replace topsoil on a flat area (the topsoil can be reused in raised beds). If you have no spare subsoil, skim off the topsoil to get down to the subsoil. Making a meadow on topsoil gives grass the upper hand. However, there is also a wildflower that you can sow that will reduce the vitality of the grasses and allow other wildflowers a way in. Yellow rattle (*Rhinanthus major*) is a parasitic plant on grassland and reduces grass's vigour and indirectly the fertility of the soil.

If your planned meadow is already a lawn, skim off the turf to a depth of about 10cm (4in). Stack the turf, grassy edge to grassy edge, in an out-of-the way corner where it will rot down to a rich, crumbly compost for the vegetable garden or raised beds.

On bare soil you can deplete fertility by growing a greedy crop such as potatoes, or courgettes or corn on the cob. Don't feed the soil and, when you harvest your crop, scrupulously clear away all vegetable waste. You can combine this technique with stripping off some of the topsoil too.

SOWING DIRECT

Once you've got your proposed area into shape, it's a good idea to wait and see what comes up before sowing a meadow-seed mix. If difficult, deep-rooted weeds like dock start to grow, it is easier to hoe them

left A typical summer meadow with ox-eye daisies, red clover, and plantains.

right Scabious ia a meadow flower and while *Knautia macedonica* is a garden species, it is still closely enough related to field scabious (*K. arvensis*) to justify growing it in an artificial garden meadow.

out when the ground is still bare rather than trying to grub them out of the midst of newly sown wildflower seedlings.

The best time to sow meadow seed is in early spring or early autumn. Many seed suppliers offer mixes to suit different soils and situations. Choose a still day and follow the supplier's instructions – usually only a small amount of seed is needed to cover a square yard. Sow the seed 'broadcast' – i.e. by hand – and rake it in very lightly in an attempt to fool the birds.

You could also add seed of annual species such as the field poppy and corncockle (which is virtually extinct in the wild), so that you get some flowers in the first year – perennials such as scabious, knapweed, vetches and wild geraniums take some time to establish. (Once the meadow is established, the annuals will gradually die out, as they are cornfield weeds that only flourish on ploughed land.)

GIVING MEADOW FLOWERS A HEAD START

Rather than leaving germination to chance, you can start off flower seedlings indoors, in the greenhouse, or in a cold frame, so that at least you can be sure of what you're planting out. If you're good at identification, sow a random seed mix and sort out the species when you prick out the seedlings. If not, buy flower seed in single-species packets.

To give the seedlings the best start, grow them on in their pots for the summer or even an entire year, until they have developed into sturdy plants. Don't let them flower and set seed – cut off any flower shoots so that all the plant's growing energy is concentrated on building up a strong root system and plenty of leaves.

Plant them out into the meadow area in spring or autumn, remembering that bees, butterflies and other insects will get most benefit from drifts of the same species, so plant meadow flowers in groups and not too far apart within the groups.

NEGLECT OR DELIBERATE DESIGN?

In a small garden making a meadow is fraught with difficulties, not least that it can look like neglect and not a deliberate design. There are various ways of dealing with this, to make the meadow a very obvious part of the garden design. One way is to mow a path through it or to mow an edge to it, so that the contrast is clear. Keep any brick or paved paths that border the meadow area clear – with visible structure around it, a meadow looks part of the grand design.

above Mowing a path through a meadow not only prevents visitors crushing too many flowers, it also indicates that this is a deliberate planting rather than a neglected lawn.

right A typical meadow mix of vetches, clovers, plantains and grasses.

MEADOW FLOWERS

Spring meadow flowers

Bugle (*Ajuga reptans*)

Cat's ears (*Hypochaeris radicata*)

Cowslip (*Primula veris*)

Daisy (*Bellis perennis*)

Dandelion (*Taraxacum officinale*)

Ladys' smock (*Cardamine pratensis*)

Selfheal (*Prunella vulgaris*)

Speedwell (*Veronica agrestis*)

Summer meadow flowers

Field scabious (*Knautia arvensis*)

Goatbeard (*Tragopogon pratensis*) –
   like a giant dandelion

Harebell (*Campanula rotundifolia*)

Knapweed (*Centaurea scabiosa*)

Lady's bedstraw (*Galium verum*)

Meadow buttercup (*Ranunculus acris*)

Ox-eye daisy (*Leucanthemum vulgaris*)

St John's wort (*Hypericum perforatum*)

Weeds and weeding

Even in a wildlife-friendly garden you will still find yourself making the distinction between weeds and wildflowers. Despite all weeds technically being wildflowers, there are some species that you still won't want to give elbow room to – species that are too invasive, too vigorous and just too successful, which will colonize the garden at the expense of other less robust but more desirable species.

Weeds can be most problematic on bare soil where you are establishing a new habitat, and there are various solutions to try. One is to prepare the soil – whether for sowing a bed of annuals or planting a hedge – and then leave it for a few weeks. This allows weed seeds time to germinate: once they have started growing, hoe them off and get on and plant or sow whatever you have planned. You'll still have to keep weeding but at least you'll have seen off the first wave of unwanted seedlings.

Mulching (see also page 100) can be a good way of weakening persistent difficult weeds like dock, with its long tap root. You can buy special membrane – landscape fabric – that allows rain, but not light, to penetrate. Use it to cover a patch of ground and actually plant through the membrane into the soil. This is a particularly useful method when starting off a new hedge. The saplings can be planted by cutting cross-shaped slits in the membrane and folding it back to make a planting hole. The membrane mulch stops weeds competing with vulnerable new saplings for water and nutrients.

GROUND-COVER PLANTING

If weeds get a foothold in one corner of the garden they can easily spread to other areas. One way of keeping them in check is to use ground-cover

left Use ground-cover planting such as the evergreen ivy *Hedera colchica* 'Sulphur Heart' and leathery-leaved bergenia or elephant's ears to blanket out weeds.

planting to cover up the soil on awkward or unused sites so that weeds can't use them as a launching point.

In a wildlife-friendly garden, one of the best ground-cover species is ivy. Ivy doesn't just grow vertically: it will cover slopes, banks and even flat beds of poor soil. It will still flower and fruit, and offer shelter to insects and invertebrates at ground level. Growing ivy as ground cover could be an opportunity to choose a more decorative variety – 'Goldchild' has leaves edged in yellow; 'Eva' has small grey and cream leaves and 'Sagittifolia' has leaves shaped like arrowheads.

Other ground-cover species that are closely related to wildflowers include a low-growing white-flowered form of comfrey (*Symphytum orientale*), which flowers in spring and has rough, hairy, dark green leaves; various members of the deadnettle family (*Lamium*) and woodruff (*Galium odoratum*). All of these are successful at covering unpromising areas, even dry shade, but need to be kept an eye on as they spread quickly and not always where they are wanted.

On acid soils, heathers (*Erica* and *Calluna* spp.) can make good ground cover. They are evergreen and some species have coloured spring foliage; bees will appreciate their flowers. On poor, dry soil, thyme can be grown for ground cover. There are hundreds of varieties to choose from, with flowers from pink to white, and green or grey leaves. Bees love the

flowers and again they are evergreen and just need a light clipping over from time to time to keep plants neat and bushy.

Periwinkle is almost as good as ivy in covering dry, shady banks, creating cover and shelter for insects and other small creatures. It has pretty mauve flowers and variegated evergreen leaves. Bugle (*Ajuga reptans*) is both wildflower and garden plant, with pyramids of blue flowers in spring. It spreads quickly by runners that make new plants, and while it does best in sun, it will tolerate shade too. Creeping Jenny (*Lysimachia nummularia*) is another wildflower/garden plant crossover that is useful for adding interest to banks and slopes, with its buttercup-bright yellow flowers and rounded leaves.

Some low-growing shrubs can be useful ground cover, especially on steep banks. *Cotoneaster horizontalis* needs virtually low maintenance and will cover an awkward site with a lovely herringbone pattern of branches, decorated with tiny pink flowers in spring and red autumn berries. It is a good bee and bird plant too. Creeping juniper (*Juniperus horizontalis*) will cope with similar situations and, although it is less wildlife-friendly from the flower and fruit point of view, it has the advantage of being evergreen and providing year-round shelter.

PLANTING DENSELY

Another way to stop weeds ever getting started in the first place, is to plant densely. This means ignoring seed packet instructions and plant label advice, and setting plants closer together. Even reducing planting distances by half will have a big impact on the amount of open space available for weeds to colonize.

The main reason that planting distances are specified is to allow plants room to grow and to give each one a reasonable amount of space in which to compete for food, water and light. If you can see that your plants are suffering from too much competition for resources as a result of close planting, it's easy enough to dig a plant up and shift it.

A dense planting of nectar flowers for birds and butterflies also means that visiting insects don't have to travel big distances to the next plant, wasting time and energy searching for food.

Planting bigger species – such as shrubs – closer together is not such a good idea, as the effort involved in shifting them later is altogether greater. Instead, use dense planting between them (of annuals, bulbs and perennials) to keep weeds at bay.

above left Ivy will flourish horizontally as well as vertically, and makes great ground cover in dry shade under trees, stopping weeds getting a foothold as well as creating a wildlife habitat.

below left *Lamiums* or deadnettles also make good ground cover as well as having bee-friendly flowers.

Plant directory

Use this selection of plants as an ideas base to build up your own choice of wildlife-friendly garden species. The directory is divided into sections covering trees, shrubs, perennials, annuals, bulbs, biennials, pond plants and wildflowers. Throughout the directory you'll find useful panels that highlight plants that are especially attractive to bees or butterflies, shrubs that produce berries for birds, and plants that make good nesting sites or offer shelter and protection.

The selection of plants is by no means exhaustive. Many more species fall into these categories and you'll find lots of regional and local variations as you start to investigate further. Just use these suggestions as stepping stones to get you started. Once you begin to realize why a plant is useful to wildlife, you'll start to recognize those qualities in other species too.

Trees

A single tree in your garden can be a mini habitat in its own right. Its leaves may be food for caterpillars, its flowers and berries can feed insects and birds, while its bark and branches can support a whole world of insects. Even the plants that grow at its feet will be dependent on the shade it casts, creating a woodland in miniature in your garden with just one tree.

Betula pendula
SILVER BIRCH
Height 20m (65ft)

With its slender trunk and small leaves, there should be room for a silver birch in the average garden. It doesn't cast dense shade and it doesn't take up much room: in return you get an insect habitat bar none – 200-plus species recorded on a single tree – and a tree that attracts a variety of birds such as tree creepers and woodpeckers. Silver birch does best in an open site on well-drained soil and preferably soil that is not too rich. Coppicing a tree (cutting it right back to the ground) in spring should result in multi-stemmed regrowth – your own mini birch glade.
ATTRACTS

Cornus mas
CORNELIAN CHERRY
Height 15m (16ft)

A small tree or even a large shrub, depending on how you look at it, the cornelian cherry flowers usefully early in the year for awakening bees and insects. Later on it produces bright red fruits which are said to be edible: few gardeners can verify this as the birds always get to them first. It does well on chalky soil and is slow-growing in general.
ATTRACTS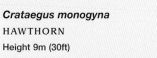

Crataegus monogyna
HAWTHORN
Height 9m (30ft)

A near-perfect wildlife-friendly tree, the hawthorn has heavily scented white spring

Malus domestica apple

Malus sylvestris Crab apple

blossom that just hums with bees and other insects. Its leaves and bark are home to a staggering number of insects (well over a hundred) and in autumn its berries form an important part of the diet of birds such as thrushes, blackbirds and fieldfares. The hawthorn is not fussy about soil type but does like full sun. If you can't afford the space for a tree, mix it in a hedge at the very least.

ATTRACTS

Euonymus europaeus
SPINDLE
Height up to 15m (16ft)

Spindles provide a curious colour clash – pink seed cases split to reveal bright orange seeds within – but this doesn't put the birds off: they feast on them. (The berries are poisonous to humans.) Spindle forms a small tree or a shrub depending on how you grow it. As a specimen it will

grow up to 15m (16ft); as part of a mixed hedge you can keep it within tighter control. Planting more than one in a hedge will also help to ensure a better berry crop through cross-pollination. In autumn the leaves colour up nicely.

ATTRACTS

Fagus sylvatica
BEECH
Height up to 30m (100ft)

Given its ultimate height, growing a beech tree as a specimen tree is going to be beyond most gardeners, but incorporating it into a hedge (see page 88) where you can keep its size under control is a viable alternative. Beech's habit of hanging onto its leaves for most of the winter makes it a good choice for creating winter roosting sites. And surveys have shown that a vast range of insects make it their home. Birds and small mammals feed on its autumn

fruits (beech mast). Beech tolerates most soils apart from really wet heavy clay.

ATTRACTS

Juniperus communis
JUNIPER
Height up to 4.5m (15ft)

Juniper's seriously prickly evergreen needles make this tree an ideal nesting spot for birds, protecting them from predators. It's not fussy about soil and will put up with poor, sandy soils and a certain amount of shade. Instead of growing it as a tree, try using juniper as boundary hedging with other prickly species, to deter intruders as well as shelter wildlife. Tiny flowers produced at the tips of the branches eventually ripen into black berries popular with birds.

ATTRACTS

Prunus institia Damson

Syringa vulgaris Lilac

Malus domestica
APPLE
Height and spread vary

Modern developments in plant breeding mean that there is now an apple tree to suit every garden, even a patio. Dwarf rootstocks keep size manageable in small gardens and self-fertile trees are common – in the past two different varieties had to be planted close by to ensure pollination and so a proper crop of apples. While some apple trees may be prey to insect pests, you will have in your garden the very birds to deal with them – and spare a few windfall apples for wasps, butterflies, birds and small mammals.

ATTRACTS

Malus sylvestris
CRAB APPLE
Height up to 6m (20ft)

Crab apples come from the same family as eating apples, but they aren't generally good to eat unless they've been turned into jams and jellies first. Birds are not so fussy though and readily feed on the fruit. Before that, bees will have plundered the spring blossom for nectar. Crab apples are small trees that can easily be tucked into a corner of the average garden or in a run of hedging. The wild species has pink blossom and red fruit – cultivated varieties come with fruit in yellows and orange, but the birds still seem to like them.

ATTRACTS

Prunus avium
WILD CHERRY
Height up to 15m (50ft)

This is a big tree with a wide, imposing shape best suited to bigger gardens. It is smothered in blossom in spring and sporadically sets fruit in autumn, appealing to both insects and birds. As the tree ages, its bark becomes fissured and cracked, supporting a wide range of insect life. As with other forest trees, the wild cherry can be incorporated into a mixed hedge for its blossom and fruit, or try the bird cherry *Prunus padus* instead. It too has white blossom in spring and small cherries in autumn but grows slowly to 3m (10ft) in 10 years, ultimately reaching 9m (30ft).

ATTRACTS

Prunus domestica
PLUM
Height 5m (16ft)

With fruit trees of any description you have to compete with local wildlife for the crop – and plums are heavily in demand from wasps, butterflies and birds. Choose a variety that crops generously and there should be enough to go round, especially as most insects and birds will make do

Quercus robur Oak

with windfalls. Plum blossom is one of the earliest fruit blossoms and may be susceptible to frost damage, so choose a sheltered spot for your tree.

ATTRACTS

Prunus instita

DAMSON

Height up to 6m (20ft)

Damsons make undemanding trees for a country garden, with pretty white blossom in spring, a light, airy canopy of leaves, and in autumn fruit that tastes like small, sweet plums. Birds love the fruit, while bees go for the spring blossom. (Don't plant a tree too close to the house – squashed damsons on the carpet are a nuisance.) You could mix damsons in with other hedgerow shrubs and keep them small by pruning.

ATTRACTS

Quercus robur

OAK

Height up to 30m (100ft)

Impractical for all but estate-sized landscapes as a tree, the benefits of the oak can still be brought to smaller gardens by incorporating it in a mixed hedge. As a result you get one of the best insect habitats that then attracts insect-feeding birds, plus acorns to feed birds and small mammals. You may even get birds nesting in oak grown as a hedge rather than a tree.

ATTRACTS

Salix spp.

WILLOW

Height varies

The goat willow (*Salix caprea*) is one of the best willows for average gardens. It can reach 8m (26ft) but can be kept smaller by pruning. It flowers early and goes on to

TEN BERRIED SHRUBS FOR TREES AND BIRDS

Cotoneaster (*Cotoneaster* spp.)

Crab apple (*Malus sylvestris*)

Damson (*Prunus institia*)

Himalayan honeysuckle (*Leycesteria formosa*)

Holly (*Ilex* spp.)

Honeysuckle (*Lonicera* spp.)

Ivy (*Hedera* spp.)

Pyracantha (*Pyracantha* spp.)

Rowan (*Sorbus aucuparia*)

Spindle (*Euonymus europaeus*)

Prunus domestica Plum

Sorbus aucuparia Rowan

produce masses of seed, which attracts various tits, tiny goldcrests and some warblers. Willows are also food plants for some spectacular moth caterpillars, and both goat willow and white willow (*S. alba*) support substantial insect populations. Trees usually do best on heavy, wet soils.

ATTRACTS

Sorbus aucuparia
ROWAN

Height up to 15m (50ft)

In a good year, a heavy crop of rowan berries will be an important factor in the diet of blackbirds, thrushes and starlings. The combination of coral-red berries and feathery pinnate leaves at the height of summer is highly decorative, but enjoy it while you can as the birds strip the berries long before winter. Rowan trees are quick-growing and can cope with exposed sites and with poor soil. They cast relatively little shade, making them ideal for smaller gardens. The closely related whitebeam (*S. aria*) is another suitable option, with silvery leaves and crimson berries.

ATTRACTS

Syringa vulgaris
LILAC

Height 3.5m (12ft)

Clusters of small tubular flowers make lilac attractive to bees and butterflies, while small birds like bluetits give branches a thorough going-over for insects. Lilacs are easy to fit into small gardens, either as modest trees or kept even smaller by growing them as part of a mixed hedge. They like a sunny spot, thrive in the extra shelter of town gardens and can cope with clay soils.

ATTRACTS

Taxus baccata
YEW

Height up to 22m (70ft)

Whether grown as a specimen tree or as a hedging shrub, yew is equally useful to birds. Its dense evergreen needles provide good cover for nesting birds and its fleshy red autumn berries are readily eaten by birds. Yew is poisonous to livestock and humans, so juniper can be a safer evergreen alternative where a hedge bounds farmland or there are children about. Yew grows well in sun or shade and isn't too fussy about soil type.

ATTRACTS

Taxus baccata Yew

Shrubs

While native species are nearly always best for wildlife, there are some ornamental introduced shrubs that come a close second and add a touch of variety to the garden. You can mix and match flowering and berried shrubs in an informal hedge or add them here and there in the border – some will even make stand-alone specimens.

Amelanchier lamarckii
AMELANCHIER
Height up to 6m (20ft), spread 1.2m (4ft)
One of the best value-shrubs in the garden for seasonal interest and one that is attractive to wildlife at the same time. The dense spring blossom attracts bees and insects, and is produced at the same time as the new bronze-tinted foliage. Then birds take the summer berries, which start off red, ripening to black. In autumn the leaves turn brilliant red and yellow. Amelanchier prefers well-drained soil and full sun, though it will put up with light shade.

ATTRACTS

Berberis spp.
BARBERRY
Height and spread vary
This massive genus of shrubs includes both deciduous and evergreen species, some tall, some ground-hugging. What nearly all have in common is berries that birds like, plus dense foliage that provides good cover for nest sites. *B. vulgaris* is a deciduous, densely branching species, which makes an ideal hedge, especially as it grows vigorously in sun or shade and on any soil. *B. darwinii* is evergreen and prickly, an ideal hedge and nest habitat.

ATTRACTS

Buddleja davidii
BUTTERFLY BUSH
Height 5m (16ft), spread 3m (10ft)
The butterfly bush barely needs introducing and if it did, the name says it all. This is one case where it is better to go

Berberis spp. Berberis

Buddleia davidii Butterfly bush

Ceanothus spp. Californian lilac

for named cultivars rather than the original species, which can be overwhelmingly vigorous in a small garden. Whether you choose deep-purple-flowered 'Black Knight' or violet-blue 'Empire Blue', you can be sure the flowers will be a mass of butterflies all summer long. Hard pruning in spring – cutting back every stem nearly to the ground – stimulates maximum flower production. Grow buddleja in full sun on reasonable soil.

ATTRACTS 🦋 🐝

Ceanothus spp.
CALIFORNIAN LILAC
Height and spread vary

Ceanothus is a wall shrub, that is it does best trained against a sunny wall, which will give it both shelter and support as well as transforming a bare wall into a wildlife-friendly habitat. Evergreen species such as *C. arboreus* provide roosting cover all year round, as well as nesting sites. Its large clusters of blue flowers appear in late spring and attract bees and other insects. Prune ceanothus after flowering to keep the size in check and to promote healthy growth.

ATTRACTS 🐝 🐦

Corylus avellana
HAZEL
Height up to 6m (20ft)

Hazels are fast and easy to grow, whether you mix them into a hedge or, if you have space, make your own hazel grove by coppicing a bush to make it many-stemmed. Their familiar yellow spring catkins are wind-pollinated, but hazels still support a wide variety of insects, which in turn are food for birds, while their autumn nuts feed both birds and small mammals. Hazels are not fussy about soil, sun or shade. For hedging, look out for plants supplied as whips – two-year-old saplings – and plant them in autumn or spring.

ATTRACTS 🐛 🐦 🐭

Cotoneaster spp.
COTONEASTER
Height and spread vary

Cotoneaster is another wide-ranging genus of deciduous and evergreen shrubs, some just a few feet tall, others making small trees. One of the most familiar and useful is *C. horizontalis*, which can turn an awkward bank or a north-facing wall into something worthwhile. Its tiny pink and white flowers are alive with bees in spring, then it produces masses of bright red berries that last well into winter and are loved by birds. Although it loses its leaves, the herringbone arrangement of its branches looks very attractive in winter. By contrast, *C. franchetii* is evergreen,

Corylus avellana Hazel

Cotoneaster spp. Cotoneaster

later-flowering, has larger orange berries and is tall enough to include in a hedge.
ATTRACTS 🐝 🐦

Hebe spp.
HEBE
Height and spread vary

This is considered by some butterfly enthusiasts to be the next best thing to a buddleja – particularly in a small garden – and in bloom some of the larger species do look uncannily like buddlejas. Hebes flower prolifically with spikes of white, pink and purple tubular flowers that attract butterflies and bees. They are evergreen shrubs, many with neatly overlapping leaves. One of the tallest and hardiest is *H. cupressoides* which at 1.8m (6ft) can be mixed into a hedge. At the other end of the scale is *H. albicans*, which rarely tops 1m (3ft).
ATTRACTS 🦋 🐝

Ilex spp.
HOLLY
Height up to 15m (50ft)

Prickly evergreen holly protects roosting and nesting birds from predators. Planted as a boundary hedge, it will keep unwelcome intruders out of a garden too. To make sure holly produces a good crop of berries for the birds you need to grow both male and female plants. Female plants bear the berries but males are needed for pollination. Observation seems to broadly indicate that birds prefer to feed on the traditional red berries, so go for common species such as *I. aquifolium* rather than fancy cultivars.
ATTRACTS 🐦 🐞

Lavandula angustifolia
LAVENDER
Height and spread 60cm (2ft)

Strongly scented lavender is a classic bee and butterfly flower with a long-flowering season. The flower spikes start to open in late spring and carry on into autumn. Traditional Old English lavender with its pale mauve flowers, seems to be more attractive to butterflies than the brighter-coloured cultivars. Lavender must have full sun and well-drained soil – it is a drought-tolerant plant. Inevitably plants get leggy and untidy after a few years and pruning isn't always successful, so have a few new plants waiting in the wings – they're easy to raise from cuttings. Lavender makes an ideal pot plant for a sunny balcony.
ATTRACTS 🐝 🦋

Leycesteria formosa
HIMALAYAN HONEYSUCKLE
Height up to 3m (10ft), spread 1m (3ft)

Himalayan honeysuckle is an introduced garden plant that birds have particularly taken to. It flowers all through summer and

Ilex spp. Holly

Lavandula angustifolia Lavender

sets fruit at the same time, and both the white flowers and purple berries are held together in long, dangling spikes. The flowering stems are quite springy and so birds tend to hover clumsily to take the berries. Himalayan honeysuckle prefers rich soil and full sun, but will cope with some shade. If it dies back in a severe winter, don't be in a hurry to dig it out: bushes often sprout back from the base.
ATTRACTS

Prunus spinosa
SLOE, BLACKTHORN
Height 3m (10ft), spread 2m (6½ft)
Blackthorn is one of the earliest hedgerow blossoms, producing its small white flowers before the leaves appear. Much later, bushes are studded with small blue-black sloes that look like small plums – too bitter for humans, but birds aren't so fussy. Blackthorn has impressive spines that make it good protective cover for nesting and roosting birds – it's a natural addition to a mixed hedge of native species.
ATTRACTS

Pyracantha spp.
FIRETHORN
Height and spread vary
Transform a shady wall or fence by training a pyracantha against it – you'll need wires or trellis to help you do this, or take advantage of its evergreen leaves and seriously sharp thorns to create an intruder-proof hedge and a secure nesting and roosting habitat. A pyracantha grown against a wall will grow taller in its shelter than as a hedge plant or freestanding shrub. Different species and cultivars have berries in various shades but, to benefit birds, go for red: *P.coccinea* and its cultivars or *P.* 'Navaho' or *P.* 'Harlequin' for example.
ATTRACTS

Rhamnus cathartica
BUCKTHORN
Height 6m (20ft), spread 3m (10ft)
Grow buckthorn as part of a mixed hedge to keep its height in check in smaller gardens. Its dense, spiny branches make an ideal protective hedge and nest site for birds, which also appreciate its prolific crop of black berries in late summer. The bright green leaves are a larval food plant for butterflies. Buckthorn is not fussy about sun, shade or soil type.
ATTRACTS

Rosa spp.
ROSE
Height and spread vary
Be guided by nature when choosing roses for the garden. Bees and butterflies like the wild dog rose flowers and birds eat the autumn hips. The dog rose (*R. canina*) has simple five-petalled flowers with prominent

stamens, followed by bright red hips, so these are the characteristics to look for. Similar species roses include *R. glauca*, which has bright pink flowers, greeny-grey leaves and red hips; *R.* 'Geranium' has bright scarlet flowers and distinctive hips with a nipped-in 'waist'. Vigorous climbing roses may not have the right blooms to attract many insects, but the well-known thorny rose *R. filipes* 'Kiftsgate', for example, makes a secure nesting and roosting habitat.
ATTRACTS

Rosmarinus officinalis
ROSEMARY
Height 1m (3ft), spread 60cm (2ft)
Like lavender, shrubby aromatic rosemary is a good bee plant and complements lavender by flowering at the opposite end of the year, starting early in spring. To make it attractive to early insects, site the

Rosa spp. Rose

plant in a sunny-sheltered spot and, to make sure it thrives, grow it in well-drained soil. For a balcony or terrace, rosemary is easily grown in a pot. Try a prostrate (low-growing) form, such as 'Jackman's Prostrate' to cloak a low sunny wall or bank.

ATTRACTS 🐝 🪲

Sambucus nigra
ELDER
Height up to 7.5m (25ft), spread 4m (13ft)
In a formal garden the elder is generally considered a bit of a nuisance – untidy and invasive – but in a wildlife garden it takes on an important role. Its flowers attract many insects in early summer, then it's the turn of the birds to feast on the berries in autumn. Unless you have acres to play with, it's probably best kept under control in a hedge. Old elder bushes can be rejuvenated by cutting them down to the ground in spring. You'll lose a year's worth of flowers and berries, but the resulting new, growth will look better and be easier to manage. On a patio or terrace, it's even worth growing one of the smaller decorative cultivars in a pot – they still produce fruit and flowers.

ATTRACTS 🐝 🪲 🐦

Viburnum opulus
GUELDER ROSE
Height up to 4.5m (15ft), spread 1.5m (5ft)
This is the native hedgerow viburnum with typical flat clusters of white flowers that attract insects in summer, followed by translucent red autumn berries for birds. Occasionally the leaves turn red in autumn too, to match the berries. Viburnum is one genus where you can allow yourself a little licence as a gardener and choose another species: for example, V. tinus flowers and fruits at the same time, and birds will take the purple-black berries – it's also evergreen and can form a hedge dense enough for nesting.

ATTRACTS 🐝 🪲 🐦

Rosmarinus officinalis **Rosemary**

Viburnum **Viburnum**

Perennials

Perennial plants come up year after year, many species gradually spreading to become sizeable clumps. In general they are low-maintenance plants, needing cutting back where specified to improve vigour, or lifting and dividing every three or four years for the same reason. Some are easily grown from seed; for gardeners in a hurry, taking cuttings or digging up part of an established clump gives quicker results.

Achillea filipendulina
YARROW
Height 1.5m (5ft), spread 1m (3ft)

The individual small daisy-like flowers of yarrow are massed together in great flat plates of colour that attract many beneficial insects to the garden, from bees and hoverflies to butterflies. Birds also like the seed. This particular species has deep gold flowers. Wild yarrow has pinky-white flowers and often grows on rough lawns and meadow areas, and has been used to breed a range of deep pink and purple cultivars. Plants need full sun and well-drained soil. Dividing them every few years keeps them in good shape.

ATTRACTS

Alchemilla mollis
LADY'S MANTLE
Height 45cm (18in), spread 50cm (20in)

Lady's mantle has small yellow-green flowers packed into tight sprays. They are not the most conspicuous of flowers but clearly attract the right sort of insects. Plants have a long flowering season and can tolerate a wide range of conditions from full sun to dappled shade. Their downy leaves catch and hold morning dew, making them a useful source of moisture. Lady's mantle self-seeds readily, building up substantial clumps and filling awkward corners in the garden.

ATTRACTS

Alchemilla mollis Lady's mantle

Aster novi-belgii
MICHAELMAS DAISY
Height 1m (3ft), spread 60cm (2ft)

Michaelmas daisies are some of the latest-flowering plants in the garden, making them an ideal nectar source for the last few butterflies and bees on the wing. They come in shades from white to deepest magenta and, as it's thought that butterflies prefer pinks and purples, it makes sense to go for those colours. Michaelmas daisies do best in a sunny spot with reasonably good soil – try not to let them dry out in summer. When they have finished flowering, leave the seedheads in place for finches and other seed-eating birds.

ATTRACTS 🐝 🦋 🐦

Aubrieta spp.
AUBRIETA
Height 15cm (6in), spread 60cm (24in)

Aubrieta has simple star-shaped flowers in shades of pink and purple favoured by butterflies. It starts to bloom well before winter ends and is an important early nectar source. Plants are low-growing and ground-hugging and are typically seen cascading down old stone walls, which offer the dry, well-drained growing conditions they prefer. Clipping over the plants tightly after they have finished flowering keeps them in good shape both literally and metaphorically. Plants can easily be grown from seed or from cuttings in summer and need full sun to thrive.

ATTRACTS 🐝 🦋

Campanula spp.
BELLFLOWER
Height and spread vary

There are lots of species of campanula, all characterized by bell-shaped flowers in shades of purple, pink and occasionally white. Creeping, carpet-forming species such as *C. portenschlagiana* and *C. poscharskyana* are best grown on walls or

Aster novi-belgii Michaelmas daisy

Campanula spp. Bellflower

banks where they can perform their best. Lift and divide them every few years to stop plants getting straggly and sparse. Taller species such as *C. persicifolia, C. glomerata* and *C. punctata* do best in sunny borders but can tolerate a little shade. Bees, in particular, crawl into the flower bells and reverse out covered in pollen.

ATTRACTS

Centranthus ruber
VALERIAN
Height 60cm (2ft), spread 60cm (2ft)
Valerian is another wildflower that is equally at home in gardens, swapping its native chalk cliffs for old garden walls or poor, dry soils. It blooms in summer, producing flower heads packed with individual tiny tubular flowers beloved of bees, butterflies and moths such as hawk moths. Cutting back spent flower heads often encourages

a second flowering, but leave some to set seed to ensure a constant supply of self-sown plants.

ATTRACTS

Echinacea purpurea
CONEFLOWER
Height 1.2m (4ft), spread 45cm (18in)
Native American coneflowers are a key species in prairie planting, the US equivalent of meadow planting. They are easy-care, prolific plants, which flower for several months later in the year and are irresistible to bees and butterflies. Part of the vast daisy family, they have purple petals with a central brown boss or cone, which becomes quite spiny once the flower has set seed. Grow them in a mixed border in full sun for best results. Deadheading spent flowers will keep them flowering for longer and so supply late-flying insects with nectar.

ATTRACTS

Centranthus ruber Valerian

Echinacea purpurea Coneflower

Echinops ritro
GLOBE THISTLE

Height 60cm (2ft), spread 30cm (1ft)

The globe thistle is a handsome plant with silver-grey leaves and upright flower stems topped by perfect spheres packed with tiny flowers of an intense, almost metallic, blue. Once in full flower, each head is rarely seen without a resident bee or butterfly. Plants actually prefer poor soil, doing best on unimproved sandy sites that are baked dry by summer sun – a boon for gardeners working in difficult conditions. Large plants can be divided to improve vigour and make new plants.

ATTRACTS 🐝 🦋 🐦

Eryngium bourgattii
ERYNGIUM

Height 60cm (2ft), spread 50cm (20in)

Tiny blue, papery flowers packed together in cone-shaped heads rather like teasels mean that eryngiums appeal to precisely the same insects too – bees and butterflies. Flowers are produced all summer and, unlike some species of eryngium, *E. bourgattii* is fully hardy and will come up year after year. Plant it in full sun on well-drained soil – the plant's grey foliage indicates it is drought-resistant and able to withstand fierce sun. Look out too for the spectacular hybrid *Eryngium* x *giganteum*, commonly known as Miss Wilmott's ghost: it is twice the height and makes a big impact in the border.

ATTRACTS 🐝 🦋 🐦

Eupatorium cannabinum
HEMP AGRIMONY

Height 2m (6½ft), spread 1m (3ft)

It's the densely packed clusters of tiny tubular flowers that make hemp agrimony attractive to bees and butterflies – they don't have to move far to have access to masses of flowers. In the wild, plants are often found growing near water – on riverbanks or beside ponds. Give them the same conditions in the garden: moist soil that doesn't become too waterlogged. Plants can become quite untidy so are best suited to the wilder, more informal areas within the garden.

ATTRACTS 🐝 🦋

Foeniculum vulgare
FENNEL

Height 2m (6½ft), spread 60cm (2ft)

Once fennel comes into bloom, its flat greeny-yellow flower heads attract a never-ending stream of insect visitors: bees, wasps, hoverflies, beetles and butterflies. Although it is traditionally grown in the herb garden, it is well worth planting elsewhere to give height to a border without overpowering it. Its stems are tall but light and airy, and the foliage is feathery and

Echinops ritro Globe thistle

Eupatorium Hemp agrimony

see-through. The bronze form *F. vulgare* 'Purpureum' has, as its name suggests, purply-bronze foliage – if you want a bit of variety.
ATTRACTS

Geranium spp.
HARDY GERANIUM, CRANESBILL
Height and spread vary

Hardy geraniums are important garden plants. Lower-growing species such as *G. macrorrhizum* create an easy-to-maintain area of ground cover, smothering unwanted weeds and flowering for months; wild meadow species such as bloody cranesbill (*G. sanguineum*) and meadow cranesbill (*G. pratense*) make useful additions to an area of long grass; while taller species still look good in the border. All hardy geraniums have pretty, open flowers that are a good source of nectar, followed by characteristic pointed seed pods (hence the recurring common name, 'cranesbill') that attract seed-eating birds.
ATTRACTS

Linaria purpurea
PURPLE TOADFLAX
Height 1m (3ft), spread 60cm (2ft)

Toadflax has flowers like miniature antirrhinums and similarly attracts bees, but because its flowers are smaller, unlike antirrhinums it's not exclusively bee-friendly: other insects can also access the nectar source. A long flowering season and flower spikes packed with tiny blooms make it a good insect-attracting plant. Plants prefer an open, sunny site and are not fussy about soil type. They self-seed prolifically so, once you've planted it in your garden, toadflax is there to stay.
ATTRACTS

TEN BUTTERFLY PLANTS

Buddleja (*Buddleja*)

Dandelion (*Taraxacum officinale*)

Honesty (*Lunaria annua*)

Ice plant (*Sedum spectabile*)

Lavender (*Lavandula*)

Marjoram (*Oreganum*)

Michaelmas daisy (*Aster novi-belgii*)

Sweet rocket (*Hesperis matronalis*)

Teasel (*Dipsacus fullonum*)

Valerian (*Centranthus ruber*)

Geranium spp. Hardy geranium

Melissa officinalis

LEMON BALM

Height 60cm (2ft), spread 30cm (1ft)

The flowers of lemon balm are what botanists tend to refer to as 'insignifcant': they're small and white and tucked away where the leaves of the plant meet the stem – and bees love them. Lemon balm flowers all summer long and grows almost anywhere, even in dry shade, though of course it blooms better in less difficult conditions. The leaves are deliciously scented but you need to crush them slightly to release the fragrance. Plants can be invasive but clumps are easily dug up when they get too big.

ATTRACTS 🐝

Mentha spp.

MINT

Height 1m (3ft), spread 1m (3ft)

To make mint into an insect-friendly plant, you've got to let it flower (something you may not have done up until now, if you're growing it to cook with). Its pretty pointed flower spikes, packed with a haze of tiny blooms, are soon smothered with bees, hoverflies and butterflies. Mint can be invasive so the traditional advice is to grow it in a bottomless bucket sunk almost level with the ground – this stops it sending out runners in all directions. If you have a pond, try growing watermint (*M. aquatica*) as a marginal plant – butterflies love it.

ATTRACTS 🐝 🦋 🪲

Monarda didyma

BEE BALM BERGAMOT

Height 1m (3ft), spread 45cm (18in)

This plant's commonest name is self-explanatory – but bee balm attracts butterflies too. It has densely packed heads of red flowers with a surrounding 'ruff' of red or purple bracts and foliage that is deliciously aromatic, smelling of the bergamot oil that is used to perfume Earl Grey tea. Bee balm does best in soils that don't dry out, in sun or in partial shade. You could try growing it as a marginal plant at the edge of a pond.

ATTRACTS 🐝 🦋

Origanum vulgare

MARJORAM

Height 60cm (2ft), spread 60cm (2ft)

This herb-garden essential is also a valuable wildlife plant and is a native of dry, chalky soils and sunny, open places. In summer, its heads of tiny pinky-purple flowers are alive with bees, hoverflies and butterflies. Later on, finches feed on the seeds. To attract the maximum number of insects, grow the wild species in preference to any cultivated herb-garden varieties. Marjoram is easily grown from

Mentha **spp.** Mint

Salvia **spp.** Sage

seed but, if you're in a hurry, it's quicker to dig up a portion from an established clump in a friend's garden.

ATTRACTS

Salvia spp.
SAGE

Height and spread vary

Sages or salvias, mints and bee balm all belong to the same family and all have similar tubular flowers, with the characteristic two-lipped shape where they open. They appeal especially to bees and to agile butterflies. In common with herb-garden sage (S. officinalis), salvias tend to do best in full sun and on well-drained soil. There's a whole range to choose from, from clary sage (S. sclarea var. turkestanica), which has dramatic pink and white flower spikes, to the azure blue of slightly tender S. uliginosa.

ATTRACTS

Scabiosa caucasica
SCABIOUS

Height 60cm (2ft), spread 60cm (2ft)

Cultivated species of scabious are closely related to their wild cousins. They all have typical 'pincushion' flower heads crammed with tiny individual florets, which attract bees and butterflies. S. caucasica has pale blue flowers up to 7.5cm (3in) across and blooms continuously throughout summer. The flower stems shoot up from tight rosettes of grey-green leaves. Grow scabious in an open, sunny, mixed flower border or in among long grasses and other meadow flowers to mimic a natural meadow habitat.

ATTRACTS

Sedum spectabile
ICE PLANT

Height and spread 45cm (18in)

Ice plants flower late in the year – often

well into autumn – in a rich burst of purple and pink starry flowers, a last burst of colour before winter sets in. Their late flowering makes them a valuable nectar source for late-flying butterflies, bees, hoverflies and lacewings, many of which need to feed well before overwintering. Succulent fleshy stems and leaves make ice plants ideal for poor, dry soil or rockeries – in heavier wet soils they may rot. Leave spent seedheads and stems in place until spring – they protect the new buds below and may shelter overwintering insects.

ATTRACTS

Solidago spp.
GOLDEN ROD

Height 2m (6½ft), spread 45cm (18in)

As a garden plant, golden rod can be one of the less desirable species, self-seeding like crazy and generally taking over the

Scabiosa caucasica Scabious

Sedum spectabile Ice plant

borders and everywhere else. Once you learn what an excellent all-round wildlife-friendly plant it is, you may be less inclined to pull it up. The late-summer plumes of tiny yellow flowers attract masses of insects and bees, while the seeds that follow boost the diet of seed-eating birds. Let it have some space in out-of-the-way corners or use it to screen off the compost heap – it's worth it.

ATTRACTS

Thymus vulgaris
THYME
Height 25cm (10in), spread 30cm (12in)
Common thyme is another wildflower that has been improved for the garden and there are many different varieties to choose from, including differently flavoured ones for cooking with. However, for attracting

insects stick to the original, with its small, dark green aromatic leaves and clusters of pink or white flowers. Thyme needs full sun and hot, dry conditions to thrive. Clipping over plants after flowering will help keep them bushy and neat, but thymes do have a tendency to go straggly whatever you do, so aim to replace plants every three or four years.

ATTRACTS

Verbascum spp.
MULLEIN
Height and spread vary
As well as the tall wild species, *V. thapsus,* with its great furry-stemmed candelabras of yellow flowers and soft hairy leaves, there is a range of smaller, more biddable border varieties that still attract bees, often with flowers that feature a strong colour

contrast between petals and stamens. *V. chaixii* has yellow flowers with purple stamens, *V. chaixii alba* is white and purple. Verbascums in trendy shades of brown and tan tend to be less long-lived. As well as bees and butterflies, plants may attract the caterpillars of the mullein moth, which typically eat the flowers but leave the leaves untouched.

ATTRACTS

Solidago Goldenrod

Thymus vulgaris Thyme

Verbascum spp. Mullein

Verbascum spp. Mullein

Biennials

Grown from seed, biennials take two years to flower. All the species listed here will self-seed in the garden. If you want to rely on a yearly show from now on, make sure that you sow seed two years running or set out small plants two years in a row. If you don't do this, you'll have a gap the following summer when year-old seedlings are too young to flower. By sowing or planting out for two successive years, you are guaranteeing continuous summer flowering by alternate generations of plants.

Cirsium rivulare
THISTLE

Height 1.2m (4ft), spread 1m (3ft)
Thistles' nectar-rich flowers attract bees and butterflies but, if in the past you've spent time cutting thistles out of the lawn, you may baulk at reintroducing them to the garden. But *C. rivulare* is a low-risk thistle, producing its small pincushion flowers on airy, branching stems in early summer. Cutting the flowering stems back to ground level often produces a second flush of flowers in autumn. Grow plants in full sun and reasonably good soil.
ATTRACTS 🐝 🦋 🐦

Digitalis purpurea
FOXGLOVE

Height 1.8m (6ft), spread 30cm (1ft)
Foxgloves are native edge-of-woodland plants, preferring a light-dappled shady spot in the garden. Their drooping bell-shaped blooms, with speckled and spotted throats, are irresistible to bumblebees, which reverse out of the flowers covered in pollen. Let the plants self-seed and you generally end up with a mix of flower colours in shades of purple and pink, and occasionally white. Sometimes clumps linger on for longer than their allotted two years, but inevitably they look tired and tatty. Plant breeders have introduced foxgloves in apricot and other pastel shades, and there are also native European species worth a try in the garden, such as rusty brown *D. ferruginea* and woolly-leaved *D. lanata*.
ATTRACTS 🐝

Dipsacus fullonum
TEASEL

Height 2m (6½ft), spread 60cm (2ft)
This spiny giant produces egg-shaped flower heads in summer, which are packed with tiny, paper,y purple flowers and popular with bees and butterflies. When the flowers have set seed in autumn, teasels are visited by seed-eating birds that feast on the narrow brown seeds, which they have to tease out of the seedhead. Teasels are true wild plants and so ideal for a wildlife garden. They do best on heavier soils and in full sun, though they may put up with a little shade.
ATTRACTS 🐝 🦋 🐦

Cirsium rivulare Thistle

Digitalis purpurea Foxglove

Hesperis matronalis
SWEET ROCKET
Height 1m (3ft), spread 30cm (1ft)

The flowers of sweet rocket come high on the list of early-spring nectar sources for bees and butterflies. The simple star-shaped flowers can be white or very pale purple and are sweetly scented, becoming even more intensely perfumed towards dusk to attract the first moths. Plants are not fussy about soil, and flower best if there is a bit of shade. In the right spot they will self-seed to form substantial clumps that please gardeners and insects alike. Caterpillars that normally feed on garlic mustard (*Alliara petiolata*) will also feed readily on sweet rocket leaves.

ATTRACTS

Lunaria annua
HONESTY
Height 75cm (30in), spread 30cm (1ft)

A good early-flowering plant that is an important source of nectar for the first bees and butterflies emerging from hibernation. Its simple star-shaped flowers can be purple or white and are held in loose spires. Caterpillars that feed on garlic mustard (*Alliaria petiolata*), and which can become invasive, will take to honesty instead, making it a good all-round butterfly plant. In autumn the papery seed pods familiar from countless dried flower arrangements are also popular with seed-eating birds. Honesty does well in sun or light shade, is not too fussy about soil and self-seeds readily, ensuring its presence in your garden.

ATTRACTS

Oenothera biennis
EVENING PRIMROSE
Height 1m (3ft), spread 38cm (15in)

The clear lemon flowers of the evening primrose mainly stay closed throughout the day, opening at dusk. Plants self-seed very successfully, spending the first year as flat rosettes of leaves before sending up flowering stems the following summer. They can become invasive but are easy to spot and pull up if you do get too many, however the sight of a flock of goldfinches stripping the seed in autumn makes it well worth putting up with a few extra plants.

ATTRACTS

Onopordum acanthium
SCOTCH THISTLE
Height 2.5m (8ft), spread 1m (3ft)

The Scotch thistle is a giant of a plant, which forms a huge great rosette of spiny silver leaves in its first year before throwing up flowering stems reaching to 2.5m (8ft) high. Even the stems are spiny. The flowers are usually solitary and are a shade of pinky-purple, attracting bees and butterflies. Plants will grow in sun or light shade in reasonably good soil. Leave the flowers to set seed for the birds and for succeeding crops of flowers.

ATTRACTS

Silybum marianum
MILK THISTLE
Height 1.5m (5ft), spread 1m (3ft)

The milk thistle is not a plant for a small garden. Its spiny stems and leaves need space. However in the right place, its typical thistle flowers, with a soft, scented tuft of purple florets, will attract bees and butterflies. Later in the year the seeds are popular with finches and other seed-eating birds. Grow milk thistles in areas of rough grass, especially on poor soil, or even with ornamental grasses in a border. Their leaves are attractively marbled with white.

ATTRACTS

Dipsacus fullonum Teasel

Hesperis matronalis Sweet rocket

Annuals

Annuals are quick and easy to grow from seed. Their lifespan is short: they germinate, flower, set seed and die all within the space of a year. The species featured here all produce flowers rich in nectar and between them attract a range of bees, butterflies and beneficial insects. Their main attraction is their flowers, making them beautiful – as well as useful – garden plants.

Alcea rosea Hollyhock

Alcea rosea
HOLLYHOCK
Height 3m (10ft), spread 60cm (2ft)

Hollyhocks are summer giants, flowering from early in the season until well into autumn, albeit rather sparsely towards the end. As well as the traditional pinks and yellows, there are also blooms in shades of apricot and the stunning maroon-flowered, naturally occurring variety, *A. rosea* var. *nigra*. Beautiful as the cultivated double varieties are, don't be tempted. Stick to the original single-flowered species that provides maximum access to nectar and pollen to attract bees. Leave the dried stems over winter – the hollow stems make perfect hibernating sites for ladybirds.

ATTRACTS 🐝

Antirrhinum majus
SNAPDRAGON
Height 45cm (18in), spread 25cm (10in)

Antirrhinums are old-fashioned cottage garden plants with colourful flowers that have a faintly spicy scent. Children love them for their flowers, which they can open by squeezing the sides, only to watch them snap briskly shut again. Grow them specifically for fat, furry bumblebees, which are sufficiently weighty to lever open the flowers when they alight on the flower's lower lip – honeybees are just too light to perfect this trick. Choose a well-drained spot in full sun and sow seed straight into the ground in spring, or start plants off early by sowing under glass up to two months earlier.

ATTRACTS 🐝

Argyranthemum spp.

MARGUERITE DAISY

Height 1m (3ft), spread 30cm (1ft)

Marguerites are ideal for growing in pots and planters for a patio garden or balcony. They are tender plants best started off indoors, then taken out on successive sunny days before finally setting them out once all risk of frost is past. Their typical daisy flowers are actually composed of hundreds of individual flowers or florets, each one a source of nectar for bees, butterflies and other insects. Try training plants into 'standards' or lollipop shapes by tying the main stem to a cane and pinching out all the side shoots as they start to grow, leaving a round-headed plant packed with flowers.

ATTRACTS 🐝 🦋 🪲

Borago officinalis

BORAGE

Height 60cm (2ft), spread 45cm (18in)

Traditionally grown in the herb garden, borage is just as at home in a mixed border. It has a tendency to sprawl and collapse in bad weather, so fence it in with a few twiggy sticks before this happens or try growing it among sturdier plants – at the base of shrub roses for example. Pink-tinged buds open to intense blue, star-shaped flowers that produce copious amounts of nectar and attract bees in particular. To keep it flowering for as long as possible, deadhead flowers as they fade – but leave some to set seed for next year's plants. Another trick is to make successional sowings throughout spring and early summer, so that new plants come into flower as the old ones finish.

ATTRACTS 🐝

TEN BEE PLANTS

Borage (*Borago officinalis*)

Thistle (*Cirsium rivulare*)

'Miss Wilmott's Ghost'
   (*Eryngium giganteum*)

Honeysuckle (*Lonicera* spp.)

Lavender (*Lavandula* spp.)

Mint (*Mentha* spp.)

Poppies (*Papaver* spp.)

Sage (*Salvia spp.*)

Teasel (*Dipsacus fullonum*)

Brazilian verbena (*Verbena bonariensis*)

Borago officinalis Borage

Calendula officinalis

MARIGOLD

Height 45cm (18in), spread 45cm (18in)

Cheerful orange marigolds flower prolific ally, the blooms attracting bees, hoverflies and butterflies alike. You can sow seed in autumn to get them off to an early-flowering start and then make a couple of sowings the following spring to ensure that you have flowers in the garden right up to the first frosts. Like many annuals, marigolds flower best on poorer soil – rich soil means more foliage than flowers. They prefer sun but will put up with a bit of dappled shade.

ATTRACTS

Centaurea cyanus

CORNFLOWER

Height 1m (3ft), spread 30cm (1ft)

Once-common wildflowers, now all but vanished from meadows and verges,

cornflowers have survived as garden plants. Their vaguely thistle-like flower heads are packed with tiny individual florets, azure blue in the original and in pastel shades in cultivated varieties. Bees and butterflies love them. Sow seed directly into the flowerbed in autumn for an early-summer display of flowers. To keep the flowering season as long as possible, make another sowing in spring. Put in a few twiggy sticks for support as the seedlings start to grow.

ATTRACTS

Coreopsis tinctoria

TICKSEED

Height 60cm (2ft), spread 45cm (18in)

Tickseed is a native American prairie flower that mixes well with long grasses and meadow species like cornflowers. Its daisy-like flowers come in bright yellow or attractive tones of brown and mahogany,

and attract bees, butterflies and beneficial insects in search of nectar. Plants actually flower better when crammed together, so making nectar-gathering easier for visiting insects. Sow seed directly into the garden in early spring: choose a position in full sun – the soil is not important, in fact, you get best results on poorer ground.

ATTRACTS

Cosmos bipinnatus

COSMOS, MEXICAN ASTER

Height 1.2m (4ft), spread 60cm (2ft)

Cosmos has pretty feathery leaves so that, although it grows tall, it doesn't overshadow or block smaller plants. Its daisy-style flowers are popular with bees and butterflies, and are produced non-stop from summer until they are cut down by frost. Deadheading improves a plant's flowering performance still further, but

Calendula officinalis Marigold

Cosmos bipinnatus Cosmos

leave some stems to set seed for next year's plants – cosmos self-seeds readily. Plants prefer a hot, dry site and fairly poor soil.

ATTRACTS 🐝 🦋

Helianthus annuus
SUNFLOWER

Height 1.2–3m (4–10ft), spread 60cm (2ft)
Sunflowers hardly need introducing, with their familiar golden flower heads on tall, hairy stems. Visible drops of nectar on the flower centres attract bees and butterflies; later on birds feast on the seeds – a single flower head can produce 30,000 seeds. As well as the traditional species, seedsmen have bred sunflowers with brown or red petals, varieties with multi-stemmed flowers and some dwarf varieties, all of which are worth growing for seeds and nectar. Sow seeds direct in the soil in early spring. If you are growing tall sunflowers, choose a corner that is sheltered from strong winds.

ATTRACTS 🐝 🦋 🪰 🐦

Iberis umbellata
CANDYTUFF

Height 25cm (10in), spread 10cm (8in)
Candytuft is an easy plant to grow – simply sprinkle some seed where you want it to flower, preferably in full sun and on fairly poor soil. It has tiny flowers in shades of pink, purple and white, which are grouped in slightly flattened clusters and can be faintly honey scented. Candytuft attracts bees and butterflies alike, and you can sometimes get a second flush of flowers by clipping over clumps that have finished flowering. Leave some stems to set seed and you are guaranteed to get self-set plants ready to flower next year.

ATTRACTS 🐝 🦋

Lathryus odoratus
SWEET PEA

Height 1.2–1.5m (4–5ft), spread 30cm (1ft)
Traditional sweet peas need a framework to climb, whether it's a wigwam of canes or an ornate wirework obelisk. Sow seed direct in the soil in autumn to give plants an early start the following year. Once they come into flower, keep deadheading to prolong the season – picking regular bunches for the house achieves the same end, as sweet peas really are cut-and-come-again flowers. Grow old-fashioned varieties for their unrivalled scent, which attracts bees and other insects.

ATTRACTS 🐝 🪲

Limnanthes douglasii
POACHED-EGG PLANT

Height 15cm (6in), spread 20cm (8in)
One of the easiest, ever annuals to grow, and guaranteed to stay in your garden permanently thanks to its success at self-seeding. The simple flowers of the poached-egg plant – white with bright yellow centres, hence its common name – attract all manner of insects, from hoverflies to bees to butterflies. The plants prefer slightly moist soil but it must be well drained: they do well along the edge of brick paths or in gravel. They are also useful in a vegetable plot where they attract insects such as hoverflies to deal with aphid pests.

ATTRACTS 🐝 🪰 🪲 🦋

Lathyrus odoratus Sweet pea

Nicotiana spp.
TOBACCO PLANT

Height 1m (3ft), spread 45cm (18in)

Tender tobacco plants need to be started off indoors and only planted out when all danger of frost is passt. Moths and butterflies can probe the elongated tubular flowers with their long probosces or tongues: some species, such as *N. sylvestris,* have flowers that close up in strong sunlight and are at their most fragrant at night, hence their attractiveness to moths. Tobacco plants do well in pots, making them ideal for small gardens and terraces.

ATTRACTS 🦋

Nigella damascena
LOVE-IN-A-MIST

Height 45cm (18in), spread 25cm (10in)

A traditional cottage garden plant that generally has blue flowers in varying shades of intensity, surrounded by a lovely ruff of feathery leaves. For a bit of added variety – and possibly more attractive to butterflies – there are cultivars that come in a range of pastel pinks and purples, such as 'Persian Jewels'. Deadheading extends the flowering period, but leave some flowers to set seed for next year. Self-sown seedlings will have to be left where they are as they do not transplant well.

ATTRACTS 🐝 🪲 🦋

Papaver spp.
POPPY

Height 60cm (2ft)

Opium poppies (*P. somniferum*) and field poppies (*P. rhoeas*) are ideal in a mixed flower border. Sow some seed directly in the garden in autumn for an early show the following spring, with additional spring sowings to extend the flowering season. As the seed is so fine, thin out any overcrowded seedlings when they germinate. Opium poppies have bigger flowers in shades of pink and purple with contrasting black stamens; the original wild field poppies are red and have smaller flowers, but also come in pastel shades.

ATTRACTS 🐝

Phacelia tanacetifolia
FIDDLENECK

Height 1m (3ft), spread 30cm (1ft)

Fiddleneck is so called because of the way its flower heads unfurl – like the head of a violin or fiddle, or, botanically, rather like a fern frond. The pale mauve flowers with dark purple stamens are irresistible to bees and a plant in flower hums with activity. For flowers the same summer, sow seed in spring in an open, sunny spot. Once established, fiddleneck should self-sow freely in your garden.

ATTRACTS 🐝

Nicotiana spp. Tobacco plant

Nigella damascena Love-in-a-mist

Papaver spp. Poppy

Reseda odorata

MIGNONETTE

Height 30cm (1ft), spread 30cm (1ft)

The flowers of mignonette are not much to look at but they smell delicious, so attracting bees and butterflies. Typically of bee and butterfly plants, the flower spikes are composed of very small individual florets of a dull yellowy-brown. Plant mignonette in a sheltered spot so that the sun's warmth releases its perfume. If sowing it from seed, sow it in position, as it is tricky to transplant.

ATTRACTS 🐝 🦋

Tanacetum parthenium

FEVERFEW

Height 38cm (15in), spread 38cm (15in)

Daisy-type flowers are favoured by insects for obvious reasons – flat flower heads to rest on and literally hundreds of tiny florets to feast on without scarcely moving a wing. Feverfew has just the right sort of flowers, but avoid growing the cultivated double form, which is pretty but has less accessible nectar. Regular deadheading will keep the flowers coming, but leave a few to set seed for next year's plants. Sometimes plants do persist for more than a year but inevitably become woody and less vigorous so, if you've got plenty of self-sown seedlings, be ruthless and pull out old plants.

ATTRACTS 🪲 🐝 🦋

Verbena bonariensis

BRAZILIAN VERBENA

Height 1.5m (5ft), spread 45cm (18in)

Technically a perennial, this verbena is not reliably hardy so is best grown as an annual – though you may be lucky and get some self-sown plants if you have a sheltered garden. Its height, coupled with its airy, open structure and tough wiry stems that rarely need staking, have made this a popular garden plant. For wildlife the benefits are small, nectar-rich flowers, and seeds and insects for small birds to feed on.

ATTRACTS 🦋 🐝 🐦 🪲

Tanacetum parthenium Feverfew

Verbena bonariensis Brazilian verbena

Climbers

Use climbers in the wildlife-friendly garden to create natural roosting and nesting sites for birds, while at the same time turning a bare fence or plain wall from an eyesore into something desirable. Flowering climbers such as clematis and honeysuckle can be used to add interest to a hedge or to cover an old shed, while providing nectar or berries for wildlife.

Clematis spp.
CLEMATIS

Height and spread vary

Vigorous clematis species – such as *C. montana* – which don't need pruning, make good roosting and nesting habitats for birds. *C. montana* also has the advantage of flowering early, providing nectar when the earliest bees are on the wing. Several species, such as *C. cirrhosa* and *C. armandii,* flower even earlier and even in winter. Larger-flowered clematis varieties tend to be less rampant so can be a better choice for smaller gardens, while the native scrambler, old man's beard (*C. vitalba*), makes a pretty addition to a hedge, with its greeny-yellow spring flowers and fluffy seedheads.

ATTRACTS

Hedera spp.
IVY

Height up to 10m (33ft)

Ivy is another all-round useful plant in the wildlife garden. Its thick stems and evergreen leaves provide cover for roosting birds and for nesting ones. It flowers late in the year, making it a valuable nectar source for late-flying insects, including wasps, bees, hornets, butterflies and hoverflies. As it flowers so late, ivy berries don't ripen until winter, often when other berry food supplies have run out, making it a valuable addition to blackbirds' and thrushes' diets. There are many species of ivy – the toughest will grow in dense shade and poor soil. Variegated species need some sunlight to keep their pattern. All are self-clinging so do not need supporting.

ATTRACTS

Clematis spp. Clematis

Hedera Ivy

Humulus lupulus

HOP

Height 5m (15ft)

Hops are native hedgerow climbers that put on massive spurts of growth, covering a wall or fence in a single season. They climb by twining, so need some kind of support system in place, be it wires, or trellis, or a hedge to scramble through. On a bare fence a hop plant quickly provides vital shelter for small mammals and birds, and plenty of hiding places for beneficial insects and spiders, improving the habitat no end. There are separate female and male plants, the females bearing the familiar papery cones used in the brewing industry. The gold-leaved species, *H. lupulus* 'Aureus' is less vigorous and a better bet in smaller gardens.

ATTRACTS

Hydrangea anomola subsp. *petiolaris*

CLIMBING HYDRANGEA

Height 12m (40ft), spread 4.5m (15ft)

Inhospitable sites like a cold, north-facing wall don't stop the climbing hydrangea from thriving. It doesn't even need trellis or wires as it is self-supporting. In full leaf, its strong, twiggy framework encourages birds to nest or roost in its protective environment. Loose heads of white flowers are produced in midsummer. Climbing hydrangea is deciduous but its brown framework can still look attractive in winter.

ATTRACTS

Jasminum spp.

JASMINE

Height 4.5–6m (15–20ft)

There are two species of jasmine that have a role to play in a wildlife garden.

J. nudiflorum is one of the earliest-flowering garden plants, its bright yellow flowers providing vital nectar for early bees and butterflies. The rest of the year it is a rather unassuming shrubby climber that needs regular spring pruning to keep it in

Humulus lupulus 'Aureus' Golden hop

J. nudiflorum Winter jasmine

check. *J. officinale* flowers in summer and on into autumn, its fragrant white flowers attracting bees, butterflies and moths. It climbs by twining, and old plants can form a dense ball of stems that make ideal nesting sites.

ATTRACTS 🐝 🦋 🐦

Lonicera spp.
CLIMBING HONEYSUCKLE
Height 3.5m (12ft)
Wild honeysuckle (*L. periclymenum*) is a familiar hedgerow climber that twines through hedges and bushes. Adding it to a garden hedge will bring flowers to the hedge, attracting bees, butterflies and moths. Later in the autumn, its scarlet berries attract birds and small mammals. Old tangled honeysuckles also shelter roosting birds and create ideal nest sites. In a small garden, try growing one of the cultivated varieties, which have flowers that are equally fragrant to the wild variety

and produce useful berries, but are not quite so bent on taking over the garden.

ATTRACTS 🐝 🦋 🐦 🐾

Parthenocissus quinquefolia
VIRGINIA CREEPER
Height 6m (20ft)
Another great way of covering a cold, shady wall and turning it into a wildlife-friendly habitat, with plenty of shelter and suitable nesting sites, is to plant a Virginia, creeper. It is self-clinging so doesn't need trellis or wires – in fact on a house wall you may find it so successful at covering bare brick that it starts growing into the eaves or gutters – in which case, keep an eye on it. The handsome lobed leaves turn scarlet before they fall in autumn, giving them an extra role in the garden.

ATTRACTS 🐦 🪲

Rubus fruticosa
BRAMBLE, BLACKBERRY
Height 3m (10ft), spreads rapidly
Brambles are all-round wildlife-friendly plants. Their arching thorny stems make great protective cover for nesting birds, their leaves are food plants for various butterfly larvae, their flowers are a nectar source for bees and other insects, and finally birds and small mammals – occasionally even foxes – enjoy their autumn berries. The drawback is the bramble's rampant growth, which makes it unsuitable for small gardens. Whenever a stem tip touches the ground, it sends out roots so that before you know where you are, you've got a jungle on your hands. In a large garden you might have room for a bramble patch, or try growing brambles as part of a mixed hedge that is cut once a year.

ATTRACTS 🐝 🦋 🪲 🐦 🐾

Rubus fruticosa Blackberry

right *Parthenocissus quinquefolia* Virginia creeper

FIVE CATERPILLAR FOOD PLANTS

Buckthorn *(Rhamnus cathartica)*

Holly *(Ilex* spp.)

Nettle *(Urtica dioica)*

Sweet rocket *(Hesperis matronalis)*

Yorkshire fog grass *(Holcus lanata)*

Bulbs

Plant spring-flowering bulbs for early nectar supplies; later-flowering bulbs are insect-friendly nectar sources for the summer border.

Allium spp.
ALLIUM, ORNAMENTAL ONION
Height and spread vary

Alliums fulfil bee- and butterfly-friendly criteria by having many individual flowers packed into one head. In the case of *A. sphaerocephalon,* they form tightly packed heads whose flowers start to open at the tip, giving the impression that they've been dipped into brilliant magenta dye. Other species like *A. christophii* have flower heads that form great globes of starry flowers. Alliums tend to flower in late spring and summer. Most need a hot, dry site and are best mixed in with other plants that will hide their rather untidy foliage.

Leave the seedheads in the garden all winter – they provide useful hiding places for spiders and insects as well as looking stunning with a touch of hoar frost.

ATTRACTS 🐝 🦋

Crocus spp.
CROCUS
Height 10cm (4in), spreads readily

Crocuses are one of the earliest spring bulbs and a reliable nectar source for early-awakening bumblebees. Their flower shape makes them less accessible and so less attractive to butterflies, except on very mild spring days when the petals open right out. Go for the more delicate species rather than the boldly coloured Dutch varieties and, if you want to deter sparrows from pecking the flowers to pieces, avoid growing crocuses with yellow blooms. Plant bulbs in autumn in a sheltered spot for flowers the following spring.

ATTRACTS 🐝

Fritillaria imperialis
CROWN IMPERIAL
Height 1–1.2m (3–4ft), spread 45cm (18in)

Crown imperials have spectacular spring flowers – orange or yellow bells hanging from a stout stem and topped with a tuft of leaves. Turn up a flower towards you and you can see great drops of nectar at

Allium spp. Allium

Hyacinthoides non-scripta Bluebell

the base of the petals which attract bees and, it is claimed, even small birds like bluetits. For best results, plant bulbs deeply in soil that has been enriched with a few forkfuls of well-rotted manure. Choose a sheltered spot in sun or shade.

ATTRACTS 🐝 🕊

Hyacinthoides non-scripta
BLUEBELL
Height 40cm (16in), spread 10cm (4in)
Native bluebells are typical spring woodland plants that come into flower before the overhead tree canopy gets too dense. In the garden, tuck bulbs under shrubs and along hedgerows to create the right conditions. Bees love bluebells – butterflies find their flower shape too awkward. Many gardens already have bluebells in, but very often these tend to be Spanish bluebells, which pose a threat to the native species as they are more prolific and hybridize freely – they are capable of overwhelming the native species. If you're planting bluebells, buy bulbs from a reputable grower and choose natives rather than the Spanish species.

ATTRACTS 🐝

Muscari spp.
GRAPE HYACINTH
Height 20cm (8in), spread 10cm (4in)
Early-spring-flowering grape hyacinths are a lifeline for newly awakened hibernating butterflies – their tongues are ideal for probing the grape hyacinth's massed tubular flowers. Most species are blue-flowered, in shades of deep navy to pale China blue, but you can also get white-and yellow-flowered forms – yellow *M. macrocarpum* is particularly sweetly scented. Species such as *M. neglectum* self-seed freely and, if clumps get too big, flowering is reduced. The best time to lift and divide overgrown clumps is in summer when the bulbs are dormant.

ATTRACTS 🐝 🦋

Lilium spp.
LILY
Height and spread vary
Old-fashioned cottage garden lilies such as *L. regale* and *L. candidum* are rich in nectar and pollen, and are favourites with bees and butterflies. Try to grow these rather than some of the overbred modern lilies which are less nectar-rich. Plant bulbs in autumn or spring, in good rich soil in full sun, for flowers in summer. Lilies do very well in tall pots, making them ideal for patio gardens or balconies. In pots or in the ground, sit the bulbs on a layer of gravel for good drainage, to stop them rotting.

ATTRACTS 🐝 🦋

FIVE SEEDHEADS FOR BIRDS

Evening primrose (*Oenethera biennis*)

Hardy Geranium (*Geranium* spp.)

Golden rod (*Solidago* spp.)

Sunflowers (*Helianthus annua*)

Teasel (*Dipsacus fullonum*)

Muscari spp. Grape hyacinth

Wildflowers

Many so-called weeds are really just opportunistic wildflowers, efficient at colonizing garden soil. So you won't need to go shopping for dandelion seed or nettle plants – you've probably already got a supply. For the visually more desirable wildflowers, buy seed from specialist suppliers or look for small plants in enlightened nurseries and garden centres. Whatever you do, don't be tempted to dig up plants from the wild.

Carlina acaulis
CARLINE THISTLE
Height 20cm (8in), spread 30cm (12in)
In the wild, the carline thistle is notable for its almost complete lack of height: it flowers at ground level in thin, rocky soil. In better garden conditions, however, the flower stem puts on a growth spurt. It has typical thistle flowers in an intense shade of purple, popular with bees and butterflies alike, though only in good weather – on cloudy days or in wet weather the flowers close up. Finches eat the seed after the flowers have finished.
ATTRACTS

Centaurea scabiosa
KNAPWEED
Height and spread vary
Knapweed is a meadow wildflower with tough, wiry stems and thistle-type flower heads with a tuft of purple florets. It flowers late in the summer and can be an important source of nectar at this time of year. Birds come for the seed once the flowers have finished. Sow seed in spring in well-drained but poor soil and in full sun – knapweed can form part of a meadow planting or looks good in a mixed border.
ATTRACTS

Primula veris
COWSLIP
Height 25cm (10in), spread 20cm (8in)
Cowslips are spring meadow flowers, now sadly rare in the wild. If you've ever

Centaurea scabiosa **Knapweed**

Trifolium repens **Clover**

planted them in a border you may have noticed how many of their self-sown seedlings appear in the lawn rather than where you intended them. Cowslips are sweetly scented and a good nectar plant. The seed is notoriously slow to germinate so for best results buy young plants.

ATTRACTS 🐝

Taraxacum officinale
DANDELION

Height 20cm (8in), spread 20cm (8in)

It does take a big leap of faith to let dandelions grow in your garden but, once you've appreciated the sight of a newly awakened bee or butterfly on the shaggy yellow flower heads, you can see the reasoning behind it. You need only a few plants – you don't have to give over your lawn to dandelions. Although their deep tap root makes fully grown dandelions tricky to dig up, their rosettes of toothed leaves are so distinctive, it should be easy to get rid of small seedlings as they grow. If the leaves look as though they have been munched by a caterpillar, let plants alone – the dandelion is the food plant of the white ermine moth. If you can bear to leave them to set seed, goldfinches and bullfinches will have a feast.

ATTRACTS 🐝 🦋 🪲 🐦

Trifolium repens
CLOVER

Height 7.5cm (3in), spreads readily

You don't really have to do anything to plant clover in your garden: unless you've been fanatically treating and weeding your lawn, it's bound to be there already, mixed in among the grass and moss. Look out for its familiar three-part leaves and let it grow rather than shaving it close. Clover's pretty pink or white flower heads are a mass of tiny, individual, pea-like florets which bees and butterflies love. In longer grass you'll get the taller species meadow clover (*T. pratense*).

ATTRACTS 🐝 🦋

Urtica dioica
NETTLE

Height 1.2m (4ft), spreads readily

Nettles are a common garden weed that spreads by underground runners. It's not the most irksome weed by any means, apart from the odd sting, and, when you realize its importance in the wildlife garden, you'll be happy to keep a clump or two in a suitable spot. Nettle leaves are the food plant of several species of butterfly caterpillar. If you can provide not only nectar plants for butterflies, but food for caterpillars too, you've created an important butterfly habitat. If you do let things slip and end up with too many nettles, dig up the surplus and steep the foliage in water to make a liquid feed for the borders (see page 97).

ATTRACTS 🐛

TEN NECTAR PLANTS

5 early-flowering nectar plants

Aubrieta (*Aubrieta* spp.)

Dandelion (*Taraxacum officinale*)

Grape hyacinths (*Muscari* spp.)

Honesty (*Lunaria annua*)

Sweet rocket (*Hesperis matronalis*)

5 late-flowering nectar plants

Ice plant (*Sedum spectabile*)

Ivy (*Hedera* spp.)

Lavender (*Lavandula* spp.)

Michaelmas daisies (*Aster novi-belgii*)

Valerian (*Centranthus ruber*)

Pond plants

Use a selection of native plants to stock your pond and the surrounding area. This is one place where it is crucial to use native plants – many imported water plants are seriously invasive and cause major problems if they 'escape' into waterways in the surrounding countryside.

Caltha palustris
MARSH MARIGOLD, KINGCUP
Height 30cm (1ft), spread 30cm (1ft)
Marsh marigolds flower early in spring, with bright yellow flowers like big buttercups. Either grow them in a planting basket supported by a few rocks or stones in shallow water, or plant them where the pond liner runs under the soil so that the plants never dry out. There are cultivated forms with modifications such as double flowers, but avoid these if you can and stick to the wild species, which will always do better and should self-seed to produce more plants.
ATTRACTS

Filipendula ulmaria
MEADOWSWEET
Height 1.2m (4ft), spread 60cm (2ft)
Meadowsweet produces big flower heads, up to 25cm (10in) across in summer, composed of hundreds of tiny white florets that give the flower heads a fluffy appearance. They also smell quite sweet. Ferny, feathery leaves and attractive red stalks complete the picture. In the wild, meadowsweet is a plant of wet meadows or ditches: in the garden use it to plant up the ground surrounding your pond.
ATTRACTS

Iris pseudacorus
YELLOW FLAG
Height 1–1.2m (3–4ft), spreads readily
Yellow flag is one of the stalwarts of the garden pond, forming thick, island-like mats that shelter all sorts of pond creatures. Grow it in the water margins or on the very edge of the bank. Its typical three-part iris flowers are produced in late spring and its attractive sword-shaped leaves linger well into winter. Yellow flag is a vigorous plant – i.e. it can be invasive – so you may have to dig some out every few years.
ATTRACTS

Nuphar lutea
YELLOW WATER LILY
Planting depth up to 2m (6½ft), spreads rapidly
This the native wild version of cultivated water lilies (*Nymphaea* species). Its flowers are smaller and more globe-shaped, with rounded petals. It is also much more vigorous and tolerant, and will put up with moving water as well as still, sun and shade, and a wide range of water depths. In fact it is so successful that in a small pond, it may be sensible to restrict it by introducing it in a planting basket to contain its roots.
ATTRACTS

Iris pseudacorus Yellow flag

right *Pulicaria dysenterica* Fleabane

Ranunculus aquatilis
WATER CROWFOOT
Planting depth up to 60cm (2ft), spreads readily

Water crowfoot is a true pond plant in the sense that it grows well and truly in the water, with its leaves floating on the surface and its roots in the sludge at the bottom. As its Latin name and simple white flowers suggest, it is a member of the buttercup family. It flowers in spring but by midsummer the show is over and the whole plant sinks below the surface.

ATTRACTS

Pulicaria dysenterica
FLEABANE
Height 60cm (2ft), spread 30cm (1ft)

The golden yellow, daisy-like flowers of fleabane are common in wet, boggy fields and ditches, making the plant ideal for the edge of a pond. Set it in the soil used to anchor the pond liner to mimic its damp native habitat. The flowers attract a variety of insects, while its soft, woolly grey leaves provide cover for frogs and other amphibians.

ATTRACTS

Veronica beccabunga
BROOKLIME
Height 30cm (1ft), spread 60cm (2ft)

Brooklime has small blue flowers a bit like forget-me-nots, and dark green oval leaves. It doesn't mind a bit of shade from taller pond plants and is best planted at the very edge of the water – either in the water itself or on the bank. As it spreads rapidly, it does a good job of covering up any bits of pond liner left exposed, and provides protective cover for young frogs and newts emerging from the pool. If you can't find it at your local aquatic plant centre, beg a few rooted stems from a friend's pond.

ATTRACTS

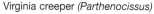

WHAT TO PLANT

10 ideal nesting sites for birds

Clematis spp.

Climbing hydrangea *(Hydrangea anomala subsp petiolaris)*

Climbing rose, e.g. Rosa filipes 'Kiftsgate'

Golden hop *(Humulus lupulus)*

Hawthorn *(Crataegus spp.)*

Holly *(Ilex spp.)*

Honeysuckle *(Lonicera spp.)*

Ivy *(Hedera spp.)*

Juniper *(Juniperus communis)*

Virginia creeper *(Parthenocissus)*

Useful addresses

Gardening advice

Royal Society for the Protection of Birds (RSPB)
UK Headquarters
The RSPB
The Lodge
Sandy SG19 2DL
Tel: 01767 680551
www.rspb.org.uk
Charity that promotes looking after the environment as a habitat for birds. The RSPB website has a whole section devoted to making a garden an attractive habitat for birds and other wildlife, with information on plants and wildlife.

The Royal Horticultural Society (RHS)
80 Vincent Square
London SW1P 2PE
To join, telephone 0845 130 4646.
www.rhs.org.uk
Gardening charity that is actively promoting biodiversity in gardens. It provides members with advice and inspiration, through education and research into plants and environmental issues affecting gardeners. The website has useful information on gardening and wildlife.

English Nature
Northminster House
Peterborough PE1 1UA
Tel: 01733 455000
Fax: 01733 568834
www.english-nature.org.uk
English Nature is a Government agency funded by the Department of Environment, Food and Rural Affairs to promote the conservation of wildlife and wild places in England. The website has useful information on wildlife gardening, with documents to download.

Bird feeders and food and nest boxes

CJ Wild Bird Foods
The Rea
Upton Magna
Shrewsbury SY4 4UR
Freephone: 0800 7312820
www.birdfood.co.uk
Manufactures the RSPB BirdCare range of birdfood, feeders, nest boxes, bird tables and accessories. Stocks a wide range of products to help you feed, identify and care for wild birds and other wildlife in your garden.

The British Trust for Ornithology (BTO)
The Nunnery
Thetford
IP24 2PU
Tel: 01842 750050
www.bto.org
Independent scientific research trust, investigating wild birds in the British Isles. Volunteers can take part in wild bird surveys. Mail-order catalogue offers bird feeders, birdfood and nest boxes.

Wildlife conservation

Butterfly Conservation
Manor Yard
East Lulworth
Wareham BH20 5QP
Tel: 0870 7744309
Fax: 0870 7706150
www.butterfly-conservation.org
Charity founded to protect native butterflies and their habitat. Website has species information on butterflies and moths.

The Wildlife Trusts

The Kiln, Waterside
Mather Road
Newark NG24 1WT
Tel: 0870 0367711
Fax: 0870 0360101
www.wildlifetrusts.org

A conservation charity dedicated to protecting wildlife in all habitats across the UK – in towns, countryside, wetlands and seaside. It has a network of local Wildlife Trusts and a junior branch, Wildlife Watch.

Wildflowers

MAS Seed Specialists

4 Pinhills
Wenhill Heights
Calne SN11 OSA
Tel/Fax: 01249 819013
www.meadowmania.co.uk

Family-owned seed business supplying mainly wild flower seed, bulbs and wildflower plug plants. Stocks 11 wildflower seed mixtures with grass, and 11 mixtures of wild flower seeds only.

The Postcode Plants Database

www.nhm.ac.uk/science/projects/fff/

Run by the Natural History Museum, this website allows you to enter your postcode and get advice on native plants that will suit the wildlife in your locality.

Bats

The Bat Conservation Trust

15 Cloisters House
8 Battersea Park Road
London SW8 4BG
Tel: 020 7627 2629
Fax: 020 7627 2628
www.bats.org.uk

Information and advice on bats. Bat-related products also available, including bat detectors and bat boxes.

Ladybirds and ladybird houses

Green Gardener

1 Whitmore Wood
Rendlesham IP12 2US
Tel/Fax: 01394 420087
www.greengardener.co.uk

Ladybirds and lacewings by post, also ladybird and lacewing houses, butterfly houses, bee houses, biological controls for slugs, barrier methods for slugs, and composting equipment.

Country Living

For magazine subscription enquiries telephone 01858 438838.

Index